THE FILM ACTOR'S GUIDE

A PRACTICAL AND CONCISE GUIDE TO ACTING ON CAMERA

TONY HART

Tony Hart

The Film Actor's Guide

ISBN-978-1-7386312-1-6

Cover design by: Anthony Hart

CONTENTS

The Film Actor's Guide

INTRODUCTION

Learning to act on camera was the hardest thing I ever did. It took me a long time to be good. I wanted to write The Film Actor's Guide to give beginning film actors a jump start, by giving them the practical skills they need. Acting can seem like a mysterious and unknowable art, but it is not. It is in fact, a set of skills that can be learned. This book is designed to teach you those skills, by boiling down all of the concepts of film and television acting into key components. The goal is to create a set of practical techniques for acting.

If you learn these practical techniques, it will save you a lot of time and grief. When I first started acting, I was the victim of a lot of flaky acting teachers, who would give me all kinds of weird advice that never really helped and only served to confuse me. I also fell victim to a lot of scam acting schools that taught me nothing, except that I should protect my wallet better. Eventually, several thousand dollars later, I learned the techniques I teach in this book and my acting became much better. These techniques led to me being taken more seriously and actually landed me more work.

The Film Actor's Guide is a book for those wishing to learn a particular style of acting, one that is the most commonly used style in film and television. That style is Naturalism. I am not trying to get you to join my cult, though. I sometimes use other techniques. I have learned the Stanislavsky System and many other styles in theatre school. My philosophy of acting: use what works. My intention is to give you skills applicable to the real world, to give you a leg up when you are getting started in film and television.

I'd just like to point out though, that The Film Actor's Guide is not a book on how to make it in Hollywood. I make no guarantees. There are many reasons why you may or may not book work. However, if you become good at acting, there will be one less reason for directors not to cast you. These are just techniques that I found useful, that made me a better actor. Hopefully, they will do the same for you.

I suggest you read this book from beginning to end, in the order I have put the sections in. I have structured it this way for ease of understanding.

THE MOST IMPORTANT THING IN ACT-ING: GET WHAT YOU WANT

The most important thing in acting is: Get what you want. What do I mean by that? I don't mean, get what you want as an actor. I mean, get what you want as a character. If you notice in every single story, drama or comedy, each character is trying to get something. When you have characters that are all trying to get something and are at odds with each other in the process, we get conflict. Conflict is the basis of all drama and comedy. This sounds negative, nevertheless it remains the basis of all of comedy and drama. Conflict is what we mean by dramatic tension. You may have heard this phrase before. In every scene of every play or every TV show or movie, there must be some form of dramatic tension. In other words, characters in conflict with each other, characters with an internal conflict, or with some other external force. Drama/Comedy is life without all the boring bits. We don't make movies, plays or TV shows about people who all work flawlessly together or succeed with no effort or struggle. That would be dull and completely not relatable. It is the struggle/conflict that makes it interesting and relatable. We all want things. We all struggle in life to get them. It is what makes us human.

When you are acting, you are "the" character. You must pursue the objectives of the character. It does not matter whether you succeed or not, that is up to the writers. But you must try to get what you want. It must be the most important thing to your character. All other considerations are secondary to this goal. Once you understand what the character wants you can then begin to understand your character. You can ask yourself, "Why does this character want what they want?" It is then that you can start doing things like building a back story, asking yourself questions about their emotional life. I cannot stress how important it is to figure out what the character wants before you ask any of these other questions. We will return to this subject later as we learn scene analysis. I mention "getting what you want" first, not just because it is so important, but because I want you to think about this concept as I explain other topics that are related.

GETTING STARTED

Breathing

First up, learn how to breathe properly. Breathing may seem a little too basic, but it will have a tremendous impact on how you perform. You must learn to breathe with your stomach instead of your chest. You need to focus on breathing with your stomach, because when you breathe with your stomach, you draw breath deep into your lungs by using your whole diaphragm. When you breathe with your chest, you are breathing very shallow breaths, only taking air into the top of your lungs. Shallow breathing makes you tense. In acting we want to start from a place of calmness. We want to be the calm before the storm. If you are tense, your energy will be all over the place. Your movements will be agitated and unclear. Your words will come out badly, you will be generally unfocused. In short, your performance will be a hot mess. Spend some serious time pushing your stomach out, and then sucking it back in to draw breath deeply. Breathe in through your nose and out through your mouth. Breathe like this for extended periods of time, and you will begin to achieve a state of calmness, or stillness. Breathing like this will clear your mind and allow you to focus.

Bad Habits

The next thing you need to do, is to identify all of the nervous tics that you have built up over the years of your life. I don't know why we accumulate these habits, but we do. For me, it was grinding my teeth together. In normal life we ignore these things about each other. Just one of the many things we sort of filter out. But on camera, these things are very noticeable. The camera sees everything. If you grind your teeth or blink too much or lick your lips (whatever it is), it will make your character seem nervous. We won't see the character; we will just see a twitchy actor. The whole point of getting rid of these habits is to give you the basis upon which to build the character. We want a blank canvas to start with. We don't want to see the actor; we want to see the character. We want to see someone who is focused and connected to the other characters. All these tics and habits we collect can distract from that. Watching yourself on video doing a scene, will help you identify these nervous habits. We must learn to be still. Then we can build the character on top of that

Connection

Another crucial habit to get into, is to be connected to the other actors in the scene. The way to connect with the other actors, is simply focus on them, and make the scene about them. Not about yourself. In a scene you will be mainly focused on trying to change the other character or get them to give you something. It is about them. Listen, when your character is not talking. Pay attention to the other actors in the scene. don't just be thinking of your next line. Much of acting is reacting.

There are those who believe that acting is putting on a performance, so they focus only on what they are doing. Putting on a performance may be fine if you're doing some kind of biopic or a one person show, but not if you are in a scene with other actors/characters, from whom you need to get things. Give the other actors/characters your attention.

A good way to start a scene, is to simply make eye contact with the other actor. Establish a connection. Then begin the scene. A good general rule in a scene, is to maintain as much eye contact as possible. If eye contact is not possible because of the way the scene is written, or the way the director has chosen to shoot it, then listen as much as you can. Form a connection with your ears instead of your eyes. As you get stronger as an actor, you will be able to stay connected without eye contact and therefore you will be able to take more liberties with eye contact. You will be able to glance away if the impulse takes you, without breaking connection with the other actors. But at all costs, maintain connection. The audience will notice if you tune out.

Energy

As important as relaxing or stillness, is energy. It may seem like a contradiction, but it is not. We want to match the energy of the character and fill the scene with energy. The actors in a scene can create energy between them by committing, giving each other good reactions and making strong choices.

It is important to start a scene on the right note. Keeping your energy levels up is vital to this end. If you take a nap before performing, don't eat right or are generally in poor physical shape, your energy levels will definitely suffer. I have started scenes without the right energy and found my words died in my throat or I was just a zombie and killed the scene before it started. You owe it to your fellow actors to give them your energy. Never forget, you are usually in scenes with other actors. Be giving.

Be Generous and Commit

Give to the other actors in the scene. Give them something to play off of. Have good authentic reactions. Make good strong choices, they can react to. Have opinions about what is happening in the scene. Give of yourself. Allow yourself to commit emotionally to the scene. You should commit and be generous even when it is not your close up. Give the other actors what they need when the camera is on them.

There is nothing worse than being in a scene with actors who are not committed or are too closed off to display their emotions in public. You simply will not have a good scene. It will be boring. It will not be engaging. The audience will not care about what is happening on the screen if you or your scene partners don't. To do a scene properly, one must hold hands with the other actors and jump off a cliff together, without knowing how high it is, without knowing what is at the bottom. The only way a scene will really be interesting, is if you are unsure about how it will end. Acting is risk. Without that risk, your performance will be bland. Commitment and being emotionally open are risky but you must overcome our natural compulsion to protect ourselves.

I will show you how to commit; how to be generous, when we discuss scene analysis. There are techniques that will allow you to have good strong choices. These choices will drastically improve your scenes.

Be In the Moment

Be in the moment. You may have heard this expression before. In common usage it just means be present. In theatre it is the same. It is related to committing and focusing. Specifically, for film acting, being in the moment means we are not thinking about the next line or waiting for the other character to finish their lines or being focused on yourself. Be in the scene as that character, your mind clear, reacting to what the other actors/characters are doing. Don't be outside yourself, directing yourself. Simply act and react according to your impulses. Following a pre-planned, contrived performance will disconnect you. You will just be waiting to deliver your lines. Reacting in the moment gives your performance an authenticity that cannot be manufactured.

Impulse

In life we are taught to resist our impulses. We are taught to present ourselves to the world in ways that will avoid social embarrassment or present ourselves in a professional manner. We are taught that displaying emotion is inappropriate. That is not true in acting. You must learn to go with your impulses in acting. This of course doesn't mean you should always act on impulse in real life. Just on the stage or the screen.

Overcoming the resistance to impulses can be difficult. To simply go with how you are feeling, to go with your gut, is difficult. We are taught to think before we speak. Thinking before we speak is a bad habit in acting. Impulse allows you to react naturally to what is going on in the scene, react naturally to what the other actors are doing.

Impulse is especially important in film. The camera is a bullshit detector. If your performance is contrived, forced or pre-planned, then it will come off so. Learning to roll with your impulses will help you through a scene more than all the preparation in the world. Your reactions and actions will just be so much more truthful. Not that preparation is unimportant. It is vitally important. You need to understand the scene, without letting your preparation get in the way when you perform.

Not resisting physical impulses is important. It can add to a scene in ways that are not written in the script. If you have the impulse to reach out and grasp the other actor's hand (for example), do it. It will add something special, something unexpected to your performance.

Physical Action

When doing any physical action in film, it must seem natural. There are exceptions of course but most of the time it should be just a normal action. If the script says, "cross the room and look out the window," then just cross the room and look out the window. Don't show the audience your action by emphasizing it. I use the window example because I have done this. I went to the window and really looked the hell out of that window, craning my neck and looking around. I was afraid my action would not be noticed otherwise. No one looks out of a window like that. They just look. It was weird because I was indicating I was looking. I thought I was acting great. But I just looked like a bad actor looking out of a window. Make it natural and do it as you would in real life. The rule here is don't show the audience the action, do the action.

There are reasons you might have to move unnaturally, for technical reasons. This can because of camera angles, making things distorted and you have to move or stand in a way that makes it seem natural to the audience but is unnatural to the actor. Usually, the camera people will let you know what to do. In such a case you must make the unnatural seem natural. This is the challenge of film and television. This requires imagination. It requires you to ignore the unnatural action and focus on the scene.

If you are playing a character that has a different physicality than you, you must explore how to make that natural. I am more of a thinky person and so I often walk with my head down, lost in my own imaginings. I mostly get cast as thugs and cops. I then have to walk like a tough guy and talk like a tough guy. Choose the points of the body where your energy should be centered. A tough guy might move more with his shoulders, standing tall, intimidating others with their physical size and power. I also get cast as historical villains. Playing an aristocrat from a period drama requires a different physicality. A more gentile stance, would be focusing on your legs and the top of your head, standing with dignity and poise. An aristocrat would not drop into a chair like a modern person would. They would sink straight down into the chair without bending at the waist. As if they were floating down. You get the idea.

Find out what your character's physical centers are and practice moving as them until it is natural. A good thing to do is pay attention to the people you see around you. Try and see how different kinds of people move. Try and connect that to who they are as a person. Be a student of human nature.

One thing, you of course should not do, is add all sorts of unnecessary physicality to a character, when it is not called for by the script or the director. Nothing will annoy casting directors and directors more, than someone showing off an overly characterized, eccentric performance. If there is no reason for your character to have a limp (for example), don't give them one. It will just distract the audience. They will wonder why you have a limp instead of being pulled along by the story. Remember, acting should look natural and easy and not look like acting.

Be Decisive

By decisive I mean, make good choices and go with those choices all the way. Don't ever, sort of do something. If the script calls for you to do something or if you've made a choice or you're following an impulse, go all the way with it. Never do anything half-assed. To quote a great Jedi, "There is no try. Do or do not." Only going halfway will make your actions unclear. Shout loudly, if you are going to shout.

Laugh heartily, if you are going to laugh. Jump high, if you are going to jump. Being decisive will make it clear. It will also help the other actors in the scene. If it is too much, the director will ask you to bring it down.

Let us say you are in a scene and the script requires you to try and leave the room and the other characters are supposed to stop you. Get up and leave the room. Do not stop until you are stopped. Either by something external, or by what one of the other actors says, or them physically stopping you. It is not your job to stop you. If you stop yourself, it will seem weird and inauthentic. If your character fails at a task and is stopped, that is OK. But you must have a reason to be stopped. Let that play out naturally in the scene. Let the other actors stop you, that is their job. Forcing them to act may seem a selfish act, but it is not. That actor who is trying to stop you will be forced to have a natural reaction and be forced to make a natural decision. They will have to take action, before you are gone. Decisive action will raise the stakes. If he/she really thinks you're trying to leave the room, that will add to the scene and their performance. It is in fact, an act of generosity to the other actors in your scenes. Decide what you're doing and do it.

Don't Play Obstacle, Play Solution

What do we mean by obstacle? Obstacle is what is keeping us from our objectives in a scene. Let say you are climbing a mountain in a scene. If you are focused on the how hard it is to climb the mountain, you will be playing the obstacle. It will not appear natural. You will be grunting and groaning and straining. It will look like you are playing to the audience. It will appear as if your objective is to show the audience how difficult mountain climbing is. Your objective is to reach the summit of the mountain. Your obstacle is the mountain itself. To play solution we must be focused on climbing the mountain. Think about finding hand holds on the surface of the mountain, look for places to put your foot. Focus on hammering in pitons into the side of the mountain. Do not think of the audience, think only of your next step up the mountain. You will look to an audience like an intensely focused mountain climber, doing their best to climb the mountain and reach the top, without falling. You will have made the scene natural and raised the tension level or stakes of the scene. The audience will be pulled right into the story with you.

If you are in a scene where your objective is to convince someone to marry you, you would not focus on their resistance to the idea- if at first they rejected you. In real life you would be focused on trying to convince them. You would need to focus on a solution to the problem to realize your objective. You might do this by choosing a solution. You could try charming them. Or telling them how much you love them and how you will always be there for them. Their resistance to the idea is the obstacle. If you are just reacting to that with frustration, then the scene will seem odd. Your reactions will not match how you are trying to convince them. Professing love with a tone of frustration will come off weird and not at all convince them. It is OK to react with frustration, but you must head that frustration off with focusing on how much you love that person as you are saying how much you love them. The target of your love will then see how much you love them. The audience will see you react to being thwarted but also see you change gears to a solution (tactic). You might think that a gear change will look weird, but it won't. If you have that moment where they see you change from reaction to solution, it will appear natural and draw the audience in. It will make it interesting to watch. It will be a significant change. We will delve deeper into objectives, obstacles, and solutions (tactics) in scene analysis.

Not playing obstacle, goes for the emotional side of acting as well. If you are required to cry in a scene, do not focus on crying. If you have ever seen someone spontaneously cry in real life, they do not simply let loose. They try to stop themselves from crying. No one wants to do something as intimate and painful as crying. Particularly in public. So, if required to cry: The objective of your character is to not cry. Play solution. Feel the emotions rise in you but then try to cover them up. The emotions of your character will be more truthful to an audience. You will also find that you are more able to cry and cry convincingly.

Focus on Task

In a scene, often your character might be doing something related or unrelated to the story but important to your character. Bagging groceries, knitting, jogging, smoking a cigarette. It is important to remain focused on this task. If you are doing it without that focus, it will seem inauthentic.

Once in a scene, I was interrogating another character. I was supposed to be asking that character questions and writing down their answers in a routine manner. I kept looking up while my hand was still writing. It was clear I was not really writing anything, and I was not focused. When I realized I was not focused on my task, I corrected this in the next take. I imagined what I was writing and focused on that, while reacting to the other character. The fact that I was focused on my task made me a part of the world of the film, making my offhanded reactions more natural. It made me seem like a bureaucrat simply carrying out their function, which is what the character was. My objective was to get information and record it, so I stayed focused on that. Then when something dramatic was said and I stopped writing and then looked up at the other character, it made my reaction much more dramatic and authentic at the same time. I did not have to exaggerate my movement or the expression on my face. I simply lifted up my head and looked at the other actor. The director was happy because my reaction was what we call a cap for the end of the scene. A good dramatic reaction for the camera to hang on, as the scene ends.

We often make the mistake as actors of focusing only on the intense emotions of a scene. People are not intense all the time. Scenes don't just start at the climax; they build up to it. Task will make your acting more authentic and provide you with a way to create arc in a scene. By arc we mean the scene starts out one place and ends in another. It will also keep you in the moment. The trick is not to be so focused on the task, that you disconnect from the other actors.

The Moment Before

The first note of music sets the tone for an entire song. It is the same in drama. Start your scene well and it makes the whole thing flow naturally. We call this first note "the moment before."

Decide before you start a scene, what is happening. What is going on around your character? What is your character doing, before the scene starts? Figuring all of this out before you start, will put you into the world of the story. So, when the scene starts and the director calls action, you have already started acting and the camera is cutting into your character's life as it is happening. It will give your scene a naturalism, an authenticity it would not otherwise have.

Let us say you have a small part as a host at a restaurant. When the scene opens, our main characters walk into the front of the restaurant and ask for a table. If you are doing nothing in particular when they walk in, it will seem like you were waiting for them to come in and deliver their lines. Not natural. However, if you are busy writing a reservation in the book or mentally dealing with a double booking, and you imagine that the restaurant is noisy in the background (often sets are silent and background noise is added later) and it looks like it is going to be a hectic night, then when the director calls action and the main characters walk in, it will seem like they have walked into an actual restaurant. When they ask you for a table, it will make it seem so authentic, especially if your first line is, "I am sorry. We are all booked up." Always connect your moment before to what is happening in the scene.

Just a warning: Don't make the moment before so elaborate that you are disconnected from the scene. Make it simple. Make it natural. Make it work.

Memorizing Lines

Never, never, memorize lines by rote. By that, I mean, do not say them over and over again the same way. Never write them out over and over. You will groove your delivery of those lines permanently. It will be almost impossible to do the scene any other way. If you receive direction to do it a different way in an audition or on the set, you may not be able to. I have seen it happen. It is the most excruciating experience, watching an actor be given different direction and slipping back into the groove they made in their mind, when they memorized their lines. It is painful to watch an actor repeat a scene over and over again the exact same way, as the director asks them to do it again and again, in hopes they will be able to give them something different. Don't be that actor. I have been that actor. Not on a set but in an acting class. The instructor made me repeat the scene over 20 times, until it was different from the way I rehearsed. It was so embarrassing. But I learned a valuable lesson.

The proper way to memorize your lines is to do the scene analyses and read the scene/script repeatedly. Once you understand the scene or script, and know the thoughts behind the lines, you will find you will remember your lines. Even if you forget the exact wording, you will be able to say what needs to be said.

If you want to speak your lines aloud, over and over, then say them a different way every time. I often sing my lines aloud but in a different way each time. That way I am repeating them but in a way that won't affect my performance.

Another good way to go over your lines (especially just before you perform) is to repeat them out loud, super fast. We call this technique, "Doing your lines Italian." It is best to do them Italian with another actor. It is a great, warming up exercise and gets your mind and mouth working together.

Yet another good way is to record the lines of the other characters, with space between to do your lines. Then rehearse by playing back the recording; doing your lines, as if it were a performance. Let go of your prep and just do it. This technique will allow you to rehearse lines without grooving them.

If you find that you are completely blanking on a line, clear your mind and wait a moment. Usually, the line will leap back into your head.

Back Story

The common wisdom on back story at one time, was to make your character's back story as detailed as possible. The common wisdom has changed since then. I would favor making it interesting rather that detailed. If your character's past is not outlined in the script, it may be necessary for you to be creative. Again, ask yourself questions. How did the character wind up here at the beginning of this story? What happened to them and how did they react? What were the choices they made to get here? How do they feel about where they are? What do they want? Your back story needs to connect with the story being told in the script. It needs to make sense for your character and the context of the story. For instance: Batman becomes a vigilante because his parents were murdered in front of him. In the Batman story we already know this. But if we did not know his back story, as an actor we might make up a similar back story.

Let us say we are playing a character who is obsessed with making money, but it is never explained why in the script. We could make up a back story that this character was desperately poor, and the other kids at school made fun of our character because of it. Our character could then have sworn to become rich and then lord their wealth over those who made fun of them. You get the idea.

Also, never forget, it can all change "on the day."* The director/writer might give you direction for a different backstory, so be open to change. Commit to it when you do the scene but be prepared to change. In film we mostly don't get a long period of rehearsals to shake things out. We often must adapt on the spot in this business. If you can learn to do that, directors will love you.

*When we say, "on the day," we mean: when we shoot it. It is one of the many confusing bits of industry jargon. When I first started, I kept thinking people were saying we were going to be shooting on another day. I thought they were rescheduling the scene and I would get paid for another day of work. Sadly, it does not mean that. On the day, can mean five minutes from now or next week. It just means, when we shoot it.

Emotion and Reacting

Almost all starting out actors, make the mistake of focusing on emotion. Showing emotion is not your objective. If you focus on showing emotions, you will look like an actor trying to show emotions, instead of a character reacting naturally to what is happening. You must always be focussed on getting what your character wants. Have the emotions and reactions; we want the audience to see them but stay focussed on solution and getting what you want. You can use a number of tools to help you achieve natural emotions and natural reactions.

One of which is good script analysis. We will talk about script analysis later though.

For now, let's get a little more basic. In real life people don't just spew emotion. Emotion is a reaction to something, that is not controllable. In real life we most often try to cover our emotions. If you have ever seen someone cry, they are not trying to cry. They are usually trying desperately not to cry. Apply what I said about playing solution instead of obstacle. Crying is the obstacle and stopping yourself from crying is the solution. Now combine that goal of not crying with still trying to get what you want in the scene. We will see a character desperately struggling to achieve their goal, despite their intense suffering, while trying to maintain their dignity. You have raised the stakes immensely. You have made your character so much more compelling. The audience will not be able to resist, they will be swept up into the scene.

You must think of emotions in a scene as a by-product of all your scene analysis. For instance, a scene in which your character is supposed to get mad. You must find out why they are mad. Scenes with strong emotions are usually scenes with a lot of stakes. So, for instance, another character calls you a name and the script calls for you to be angry. You must find out why you are so angry. Was the name they called you personal to your character? If they called your character a coward and your character has spent their whole life running from their problems, it might strike a nerve. Anger is often a reaction to being hurt. We choose to feel anger rather than the pain because we feel it makes us strong and not weak. Something to keep in mind about human nature.

In the Stanislavsky System, actors use "As Ifs," if they are having trouble connecting to the character's emotions. Sometimes the character's experience is outside our own experience. In that case you can compare it to something in your life. If your character's father died and there are all kinds of unresolved issues between them, and this situation has never happened to you, try an As If. It is As If one of your parents died and you had never told them you loved them. Or you can use it to compare the experience of the character to a similar experience in your life. It is As If, when your grandfather died. Your grandfather dying is not the same thing, but it is a start. It might give you an idea of the emotional stakes and let you connect emotionally to the scene. It is very important not to use the As If technique while performing the scene. Only as part of preparation. The audience will be able to see that your emotions do not match the context of the scene. It is also important for your mental health to not dredge up intimate feeling from your own life, in public.

Again, it is important not to force emotions. They will come if you just do your scene analysis, commit to the scene and react.

Relationship

It may be useful to think about what sort of relationship your character has to the other characters in the script. What sort of dynamic exists? I do not necessarily mean this literally. You may have a literal mother daughter relationship between your character and another. That relationship is self-explanatory. But there may be times when your character may have a literal relationship that feels like a different kind of relationship.

In *Star Wars*, Luke and Ben Kenobi have a student/master relationship. However, there may be a father son quality to it as well. Luke never had a real father in his life and Ben is an older male offering him the guidance a father might give. This dynamic creates a similar but not literal father son relationship. In Aliens Ripely and Newt aren't related. Both have lost any family they had. They naturally form an almost mother daughter relationship. Or a big sister, little sister relationship. Thinking about relationship in a non literal way, may offer you guidance on what the dynamics of a relationship are and add more emotional stakes to a scene, as well as adding interesting layers to a performance. Within a scene a relationship dynamic may change and even flip. Watch for these in the beats (changes) of the scene. We will discuss beat changes later.

Playing Small Roles

When you start out, you will be playing quite a lot of small roles. Small roles are tricky because you usually have so little information to work with. If you are playing a bellhop with one line, it is difficult to prepare for.

Many people will tell you that small roles are the most challenging. They will tell you to do even more work than for a larger role. Create an enormous back story, really delve into the bellhop's motivations, spend time figuring out physicality. Being this elaborate is a waste of time and will almost ensure you don't get the role. If you make a big deal out this small character, it will look weird and unnatural. Bell hops don't do their jobs with their emotional baggage on display. Make it simple and make it work.

If you are being cast in a small role, it is because you look like the character. Casting is done this way so the audience gets who you are, in the few seconds you might be on screen. Just play yourself as if you were a bellhop, waiter, cop number1, etc... Don't mess with subtext. That way it will be natural and believable. Your objectives should be simple and literal. If you are Bell Hop #1, take the guests luggage and politely take them to their room. If you must have a back story, make it simple. Like you are doing this job to pay your way through college. Have opinions if required but cover them with the politeness we show to strangers.

Doing little preparation for small roles, could be wrong, depending on the script. There are the odd small roles that really matter and must be prepared for in a complex manner. They are rare though. Most of the time these roles are about playing profession or a random stranger. Make it simple. Make it work.

Dealing With Stage Fright/Performance Anxiety

All of us start acting with varying degrees of self-confidence. I have met people who were extremely comfortable performing, the first time they acted. Others are very nervous, like I was when I started. The only way to overcome stage fright, is to force yourself to do things in public. One thing that really helped me was karaoke. It might also work for you. Find a busy karaoke bar and sing songs but sing them really badly. I mean sing off key, too loudly, really sing to fail. Have fun doing it too. If you fail in public, over and over again, you will get used to it. You will not be so nervy. Then start trying to get better at singing, really try to improve. After a while you will train yourself to deal with public failure by focusing on your skill. You will begin to focus on what you are doing wrong in an objective manner. You will not be freaking out. That is exactly what confidence is. That is where we want to be as actors.

You could try this with any form of public performance. just as long as you get used to failure. Acting is risk. We do not always succeed. The failure part is not important. What is important is how we react to failure.

Acting Classes

Just a brief note on acting classes. Shop around a bit before you commit to one. In my experience the best ones are on-going scene work classes. An "on-going" scene work class is a class where you are given a scene to prepare and then film it in class. The scene is watched, critiqued and then you usually re-film it the next class, applying what you learned in the critique. Usually these schools have beginner, intermediate and advanced classes. It may take some trial and error before you find a good one. Often the local acting union will have a list of schools. There are lots of scammy schools that are just interested in taking as much money from you as they can. Also, beware of acting schools that teach obscure techniques of acting, or blend spiritualism into their teaching. You want an instructor that gives direct and practical techniques. Not someone that will just confuse you; wasting your time and money. Make sure the instructor is a currently working actor. If you want to be a professional, then learn from a professional. These classes will accelerate your skill development and give you valuable acting experience. At the same time, try to audition and act as much as possible. Experience is the best teacher.

SCENE AND SCRIPT ANALYSIS

Arc

When you analyze a scene (or an entire script), it is important to understand that characters start out one place and end up another. They have an arc. Knowing about arc will help prevent your performance from being flat. A great example of arc is *The Godfather*. At the beginning of the movie Michael is trying to live a normal life and escape the underworld his family operates in. Then his father is shot. He realizes that he must take control of his family, to save them from their enemies. By the end of the film, he has done such a good job of fighting off his family's enemies, that he has become a ruthless monster. Characters, to be interesting, must change. Michael is interesting because he is a decent man trying to do the right thing but winds up becoming a gangster in the end. Find out how your character changes and you will make your performance very gripping for the audience.

Scenes also have an arc. Try and find the arc in the scene you are in. Figure out where you are at the end of a scene and try to start as far away from that place as possible. Where to start a scene and where to finish, also depends on where your character is in the overall story. However, it is a good general rule. The arc can be discovered in the text. From the dialogue, you will be able to tell if your character is succeeding or failing in their goals. They may start out as far away from succeeding as possible, then by the end they might very well get what they want. They may even change what they want to get.

Find the beats in the scene, the places where a change happens. A beat may signify a tactic change. You might start out trying to ask another character for something politely and end it by trying to intimidate them into giving you what you want. Interesting scenes usually change. Beats can also come at the end of a scene. Your character may fail to get what they want, or they may succeed. Either way, have an opinion about it. The viewer will see that opinion in your eyes, in your physical reactions. Strong opinions or reactions can be achieved by discovering the stakes in the scene. Ask yourself what your character gains if they succeed or loses if they fail. If the stakes are high then win, lose, or draw it will add a large emotional arc to the scene.

Do not play the ending of a scene throughout the whole scene. Whether your character succeeds or fails in the end, do not play that up front. Before the scene, you can take yourself through the emotions that character feels at the end of the scene, to warm up emotionally, but let it go before you start. If you do not let it go, your scene will have only one note. It will start and end the same way. No arc. Not interesting. Start far away from where you end.

Components of Arc:

- What does your character want?

- Where do they wind up at the end?

- Where does the character start out?

- What tactics do they use to get what they want?

- Where are the beats and what do they mean?

- Do the beats suggest a tactic change?

- Do the beats suggest an objective change?

- Make your tactics about changing the other character in the scene.

- What are your characters opinions about what is happening in the scene?

- Does their opinion change?

- Do they succeed in achieving their objective?

Stakes

Stakes, a very important concept in drama and comedy. The stakes of a scene or story will determine how intense the scene is, how important it is. Stakes will determine the emotional character of a scene. They are what your character has to gain or lose in a scene, film, or a whole series arc. In other words, how important is it to achieve their objective.

If a director asks you to be more intense, or bigger and you are having trouble doing that, just raise the stakes. Make it about life or death. Make your character's objective the most important thing to them on earth. If that is too much, then select something in between. Make it something drastically important, but something that fits with the scene and overall story. But remember, be specific. Gaining the love of your life and succeeding at your career can be equal in stakes (depending on the character) but they will play very differently on camera. Asses specifically what kind of stakes there are for your character in the scene, and the over all story.

Stakes can also change within the story itself. Watch for that when you read scripts. In Star Wars, at the beginning, Luke wants to be a pilot and a Jedi more than anything on earth. He wants to join the rebellion. For him the stakes are giving his life meaning, finding a purpose, realizing his dream. As the story goes on it becomes about rescuing the princess. Then it becomes about destroying the Death Star. Billions will die if he fails. The stakes went from personal fulfillment to saving a life; to the deaths of billions. That is a rather large change in stakes.

Read every scene with stakes in mind. Ask what the stakes are and if they change. This will get you to the right emotional intensity without forcing it. The emotion will just happen if you commit to the stakes. Let go of your feelings and it will happen. I know this is difficult to do. It requires trusting yourself. Turn off your targeting computer and trust yourself (Star Wars reference). In other words, turn your thinking off and trust yourself, trust the process. When acting is done right, it seems easy. You don't have to work hard to show emotion when you trust yourself and the process. The intensity and emotion will come if you understand the stakes.

Beat Changes

"Beats" or "beat changes" are the points in a scene where a change happens:

- A character changes their tactics after failing to achieve their objective

- A character has a significant realization

- A character gives into the wishes and desires of another character

- A character makes a big decision

- A character changes their opinion about someone or something

- What the character wants, changes

I am sure there are Many more examples, but these are probably the most common. Change is the operative word here. Scenes where nothing changes are usually not very interesting scenes. Movies and TV shows where nothing changes are usually quite boring. We don't make movies about people who have no opinions, make no decisions, never change and never try to get anything.

An example of a major beat change would be the ending of *Jerry Maguire* when Tom Cruise realizes he is in love with Renée Zellweger. Another beat change is when he decides to go out on his own and leave the agency he is with. Or the moment Renée Zellweger decides to leave with him. In *The Godfather*, the moment Michael Corleone volunteers to go to the negotiations with his fathers' enemies and kill them, is a major beat change. It is the moment where everything changes for Michael. Some beat changes are so big they change the course of the story. Other beat changes are minor.

In these beat changes we have to see the change in the actors' eyes and body language. Do not try and fake a beat change. Focus on the choice your character is making. In *The Godfather* example, you would focus on trying to achieve the goal of protecting your family. In that moment you must decide that you are willing to become a murderer to accomplish this end. For a character like Michael, it becomes the most significant choice of his life. It changes who he is as a person. If we see the character coming to this decision, realizing that he is the least likely to be suspected of violence or treachery, realizing that he is the only one that can pull off their plan. If we as audience see the thought process in you, you will have accomplished acting greatness.

Objectives, Obstacles and Tactics (Solutions)

When you start analyzing a scene, you must assess what your character is trying to get- their objective. Usually in drama and comedy, this means changing the person or people you are in the scene with. It could be changing their minds about something, changing their opinion about you or someone else, trying to get them to give you something. You must assess what your obstacles are and then select the right tactic or solution to overcome that obstacle and achieve your objective. The tactic must fit in the context of the scene.

As an actor we want to be excellent and make our performance unique. Therefore, we must be very specific in our tactics. Being specific is key to understanding what we are doing in a scene and avoiding generalized performances. A good exercise that helps, is to choose a Transitive Action Verb, a verb or action designed to transform or change someone. They can help you hone your performance to a much finer edge and make it unique. Let us say you are in a scene where you are asking someone for help (your objective). Your obstacle might be that your character has been dishonest in the past and the other character in the scene does not trust you. Your line of dialogue is, "I know I haven't always been honest, but I have changed. Please help me." We could choose the tactic, "to be honest to her," "or to beg her," but those are general. Besides, you can be honest without being sorry. If we choose the tactic, "confess to her," then it is way more specific. You are not just being honest; you are asking for forgiveness. Confession is not just about changing ourselves, it is about changing and asking someone for forgiveness, to change their perception of you. Confessions always involve more than one person. That is way more powerful and way more interesting. Your line then carries so much more meaning. You will also be able to connect emotionally with the lines in a much more powerful way. You will have the audience's attention. It will be much more believable if the other character, then helps you.

If the writers went the other way and the other character does not help you, after your heart felt confession, then it is much more gut wrenching. Either way, you have raised the stakes and made the scene more compelling.

At the back of the book is a list of some Transitive Action Verbs. Try practising scenes with other actors and experiment with different transitive action verbs. You can also do improvised scenes with other actors after drawing a random objective and Transitive Action Verb out of a hat. These exercises will make you more flexible as an actor and make your performances more specific and memorable. Also, whenever you can, expand your vocabulary. It gives you an edge as an actor.

Often tactics will change in a scene, so watch for that. A tactic change usually means that the first tactic failed, and your character needs to try a new one. At first, you may be calmly trying "to convince" another character to your character's point of view. Halfway through the scene it may become apparent, from your character's dialogue, that you are trying to "coerce" the other character. Probably because the tactic of calm persuasion failed. If the "coercion" fails, then it might change again to, "appealing to them." The trick is to identify in the scene where there is a beat change that results in a change of tactics.

Opinions (Reactions)

When you're acting in a scene, allow yourself to have opinions about what the other character is doing or saying in the scene. We have opinions in real life. We may have to cover up those opinions, but we do have them. Opinions will help you react truthfully in a scene and (if the script is well written) will make your words have more meaning. They will make your beat changes make sense. When something happens in a scene, or is said, ask yourself how your character feels about it. Don't force it though. If you have the opinion, we will see it in your eyes, your physicality. Just follow your impulses.

Your character, also may have to cover their opinions up too, depending on the scene. Just like in real life, we don't express all of our opinions in the moment. The audience still must see those opinions. The trick is to show them a bit and then cover them.

Scene Analyses

Now that we have some tools in our toolbox, lets get down to business. Scene analyses is the key to good acting. It will help you understand what your character wants, what their obstacles are, and how they are trying to get what they want. It is particularly crucial for auditions, as often you only have a scene and a one sentence outline of the part you are auditioning for. You must mine the text of the scene for as much information as possible. Do not stop analyses of the scene, until there are no more questions in your mind about the scene.

There are different techniques for doing script analysis. Some people just read the script over and over until they feel they understand it. The technique I use is a little different. Before I even read the scene, I print it off and cover it with a sheet of blank paper. Then I move the blank paper down line by line and write down the following:

- On the left-hand side of the page, beside each of my character's actions and dialogue, I write what objective I am trying to accomplish (what I am trying to get).

- Under my objective I write specifically what I want the other character to do and/or what I want them to say. This gives me an expectation to be either met or not by the other character.

- On the right-hand side, I write down how I am going to get what I want from them (tactic). I do this in the form of a transitive action verb.

- Under each of the other character's actions and dialogue, I write my opinion (feelings) about what they have done or said.

Do not carve your choices in stone as you may discover a better way as you analyze, or when you actually do the scene. Remember, go with your impulses and instincts when performing. When you are trying to get what you want from the other character, read your actions, and dialogue and figure out how you are getting what you want. Find a specific transitive action verb that describes it. Remember, generality is bad.

In the following scene, we are playing Keller, a new detective on the squad.

Let's move the sheet down so we can see the first line of text.

INT. MAJOR CASE SQUAD - DAY

INT. MAJOR CASE SQUAD - DAY

This first line of text is called a "scene heading." We can see from the scene heading that we are inside. INT means interior (EXT means exterior). We are in the Major Case Squad, and it is daytime. We now have a sense of space and time for us to inhabit. We know from Major Case Squad; we are in an office full of elite police. Without knowing anything else, we can glean from this location that it is probably a police drama. We know from Major Case: that we are in a high-pressure environment and the stakes are probably high. So let us just jot down "Elite Police" next to the scene heading. We are simply noting Elite Police, as it may raise the stakes.

INT. MAJOR CASE SQUAD - DAY Elite Police

Let's move the paper down again, until we see the next line of text.

INT. MAJOR CASE SQUAD - DAY Elite Police

Harrington plops down into his seat at his desk. Keller follows. Harrington points at the desk across from his.

We see that it is an action slug. An action slug is used to describe a scene or describe physical action. From this slug we know two people walk in. One points to the desk. Nothing is said. Already we have a tone for the scene. It is tense. Harrington's actions are rude. He is literally telling Keller to sit. Under this action slug, let us write down our opinion as Keller. Be specific about this opinion. We are annoyed, but why are we annoyed? We are annoyed because it is a bit "demeaning" to be told to sit with a rude gesture. So let us write that down.

INT. MAJOR CASE SQUAD - DAY *Elite Police*

Harrington plops down into his seat at his desk. Keller follows. Harrington points at the desk across from his. *Demeaned*

Moving the sheet down to the next line of text, an action slug.

INT. MAJOR CASE SQUAD - DAY *Elite Police*

Harrington plops down into his seat at his desk. Keller follows. Harrington points at the desk across from his. *Demeaned*

Keller sits down.

We see Keller sits down. Why do we sit down? Why aren't we challenging Harrington? The fact that we accept his disrespect, indicates some sort of power dynamic. We don't really know the nature of this power dynamic yet. So, let's write down "Pissed but accepts" under this slug.

```
INT. MAJOR CASE SQUAD - DAY  Elite Police

Harrington plops down into his seat at his
desk. Keller follows. Harrington points at
the desk across from his. Demeaned

Keller sits down. Pissed but accepts.
```

Let's move the sheet down again.

```
Harrington plops down into his seat at his
desk. Keller follows. Harrington points at
the desk across from his. Demeaned

Keller sits down. Pissed but accepts.
               KELLER
          You don't have to worry
          about me. I am a
          competent and driven
          detective.
```

The next bit of text is Keller, our first line of dialogue. From the dialogue we can see we are trying to reassure him about our abilities as a detective. Why are we reassuring him? Perhaps we want to gain his approval or acceptance, as we are new to the squad. We do not know what happened before this scene, but it is clear Harrington is an obstacle to our acceptance on the squad. Perhaps Harrington doubts Keller's abilities as a detective. Then the obstacle is Harrington's doubt. Our objective is to gain acceptance and we are doing it by assuring him. On the left margin we write down "Acceptance" and on the right margin we write down "Assure him." The left margin is our objective and the right our tactic. Our tactic should be in the form of a transitive action verb. We use a transitive action verb because we are trying to change the other person in some way. Under acceptance it might be useful to also write what specifically, you want the other character to say or do. Let's write down that we want him to say "Sorry, welcome to the squad."

Harrington plops down into his seat at his
desk. Keller follows. Harrington points at
the desk across from his. *Demeaned*

Keller sits down. *Pissed but accepts.*

KELLER

Acceptance You don't have to worry *Assure him.*
             about me. I am a
Sorry, welcome to competent and driven
the squad.   detective.

Moving the sheet down again we see another action slug, describing
a text Harrington receives.

Keller sits down. *Pissed but accepts.*

KELLER

Acceptance You don't have to worry *Assure him.*
             about me. I am a
Sorry, welcome to competent and driven
the squad.   detective.
             Harrington's TEXT ALERT goes off. He pulls
             out his phone.

He looks at his phone while we are trying to have serious discussion.
We do not see the text. Under this slug write your opinion of this an-
noying text. Let us say, we as Keller, are "Peeved" by this distraction.
Peeved is good, because it is a kind of annoyed that is specific to
something mundane and normal but can snowball with our annoyance
at being treated badly.

Keller sits down. *Pissed but accepts.*

KELLER

Acceptance You don't have to worry *Assure him.*
             about me. I am a
Sorry, welcome to competent and driven
the squad.   detective.
             Harrington's TEXT ALERT goes off. He pulls
             out his phone. *Peeved*

Moving the sheet down, we come to Harrington's first bit of dialogue.

```
                    KELLER              '
Acceptance      You don't have to worry    Assure him.
                about me. I am a
Sorry,welcome to competent and driven
the squad.      detective.
            Harrington's TEXT ALERT goes off. He pulls
            out his phone.  Peeved
                    HARRINGTON
            That's great. Did you put
            that on your college
            application?
```

Obviously, he is being insulting in a sarcastic way. More specifically we might say he is ridiculing us. Let's write down our opinion of this insult under the slug. "Insulted." We skip the super (a super is on screen text) of Harringtons text as we do not see it.

```
                    KELLER              '
Acceptance      You don't have to worry    Assure him.
                about me. I am a
Sorry,welcome to competent and driven
the squad.      detective.
            Harrington's TEXT ALERT goes off. He pulls
            out his phone.  Peeved
                    HARRINGTON
            That's great. Did you put
            that on your college
            application?Insulted
```

Moving the sheet down again we see that Keller has more dialogue.

```
                    HARRINGTON
            That's great. Did you put
            that on your college
            application?Insulted
            SUPER: Jones: We're searching the vic's
            apartment. 230 Market St. Apt. 703.

                    KELLER
            Could we skip all the new
            person BS and just go
            over your active cases?
```

Clearly, from Harrington's response, our tactic has failed. We now know Harrington is a very big obstacle to our objective. In our next bit of dialogue, we are asking him to skip the BS and get down to work, a beat that indicates a change of objective as well as tactic. We are choosing to not react with anger at being insulted. Perhaps we are just trying to get him to live with us, even if he can't accept us. We are "Settling for less." How are we trying to accomplish this new objective? We might try "Professionalize him." Maybe we want him to say, "Fine, lets get on with it." Make it about the job. Write that down.

```
                    HARRINGTON
              That's great. Did you put
              that on your college
              application? Insulted
          SUPER: Jones: We're searching the vic's
          apartment. 230 Market St. Apt. 703.

                      KELLER
   Settling for less. could we skip all the new Professionalize
      Fine, lets get    person BS and just go
      on with it.       over your active cases?    him.
```

The next lines of text are an action slug. Harrington is reaching for the desk drawer. Maybe he is going to pull out his case files. Then he stops.

```
                    HARRINGTON
              That's great. Did you put
              that on your college
              application? Insulted
          SUPER: Jones: We're searching the vic's
          apartment. 230 Market St. Apt. 703.

                      KELLER
   Settling for less. could we skip all the new Professionalize
      Fine, lets get    person BS and just go
      on with it.       over your active cases?    him.
              Harrington reaches down to unlock his desk
              drawer, then stops himself.
```

Let's write down an opinion about that. "Finally." Then he stops himself. "What now?"

```
                    HARRINGTON
              That's great. Did you put
              that on your college
              application? Insulted
         SUPER: Jones: We're searching the vic's
         apartment. 230 Market St. Apt. 703.

                     KELLER
Settling for less. could we skip all the new Professionalize
 Fine, lets get    person BS and just go
                   over your active cases?    him.
 on with it.
              Harrington reaches down to unlock his desk
              drawer, then stops himself.
                  Finally          What now?
```

Moving down, Harrington has more dialogue.

```
                     KELLER
Settling for less. could we skip all the new Professionalize
 Fine, lets get    person BS and just go
                   over your active cases?    him.
 on with it.
              Harrington reaches down to unlock his desk
              drawer, then stops himself.
                  Finally          What now?
         Beat

                    HARRINGTON
              You're right. I'm sorry.
              Why don't you grab a copy
              of the files from
              Evidence and I will make
              some phone calls. When
              you get back I will bring
              you up to speed. Sound
              good?
```

He apologizes and asks us to grab a copy of the case files from the Evidence Room and tells us that he will bring us up to speed. What is our opinion of this sudden change of attitude? This change of attitude is a major beat change in the scene. It is even written in the script. Sometimes film and TV writers do that. We could write down our opinion as, "Hopeful of Acceptance." Our previously abandoned objective is back on the table.

```
                    KELLER
```
Settling for less. could we skip all the new *Professionalize*
Fine, let's get   person BS and just go
on with it.   over your active cases?   *him.*
```
          Harrington reaches down to unlock his desk
          drawer, then stops himself.
```
Finally   *What now?*
```
Beat
```

```
                    HARRINGTON
          You're right. I'm sorry.
          Why don't you grab a copy
          of the files from
          Evidence and I will make
          some phone calls. When
          you get back I will bring
          you up to speed. Sound
          good?
```
Hopeful of acceptance.

Flipping over to the next page, we have Keller dialogue.

```
                                                    2.



                    KELLER
          Sure. Where is the
          Evidence Room?
```

Here we are just trying to, "Get directions." Let's write that down. How we are doing it, is asking. So, let's write it in a transitive action verb. "Querying him." What we want him to say or do, is just, "Give directions."

```
                                                    2.


```
Get directions.   KELLER   *Querying him.*
Give directions.   Sure. Where is the
                            Evidence Room?

Next is an action slug.

2.

Get directions.   KELLER   Querrying him.
Give directions. Sure. Where is the
                  Evidence Room?
              Keller gets up.

Then she gets up, an action that is really part of the "Get directions," objective. Sometimes in life we use physical action to prompt others to action. Let's write "Get directions," again as objective and "Prompt him," for our transitive action verb.

2.

Get directions.   KELLER   Querrying him.
Give directions. Sure. Where is the
                  Evidence Room?
Get directions.Keller gets up. Prompt him

Next, we have dialogue from Harrington.

Get directions.   KELLER   Querrying him.
Give directions. Sure. Where is the
                  Evidence Room?
Get directions.Keller gets up. Prompt him
                    HARRINGTON
              Just back there. End of
              the hall on the left.
              Tell Sergeant Powaschuck
              I sent you.

He tells us to go down the hall to the records office. Our opinion of his directions could be "Relief. Maybe Harrington isn't so bad." Because he is cooperating. Write that down.

KELLER
Get directions. Sure. Where is the   Querrying him.
Give directions. Evidence Room?
Get directions.Keller gets up. Prompt him

HARRINGTON
Just back there. End of
the hall on the left.
Tell Sergeant Powaschuck
I sent you.
Relief. Maybe Harrington isn't so bad.

Next is an action slug of Harrington pointing to the hallway.

KELLER
Get directions. Sure. Where is the   Querrying him.
Give directions. Evidence Room?
Get directions.Keller gets up. Prompt him

HARRINGTON
Just back there. End of
the hall on the left.
Tell Sergeant Powaschuck
I sent you.
Relief. Maybe Harrington isn't so bad.
He points down the back hall then picks up
the phone and dials.

Our opinion of his physical action could be the same as above. It is part of the same thing. Or we might try to raise the stakes here, subtly. We could increase the stakes by degrees. Write: "Accepted." We essentially have won. Maybe add, "I won," to raise the stakes even more.

KELLER
Get directions. Sure. Where is the   Querrying him.
Give directions. Evidence Room?
Get directions.Keller gets up. Prompt him

HARRINGTON
Just back there. End of
the hall on the left.
Tell Sergeant Powaschuck
I sent you.
Relief. Maybe Harrington isn't so bad.
He points down the back hall then picks up
the phone and dials. Accepted. I won.

Next, there is an action slug.

```
                    HARRINGTON
              Just back there. End of
              the hall on the left.
              Tell Sergeant Powaschuck
              I sent you.
```
Relief. Maybe Harrington isn't so bad.
```
              He points down the back hall then picks up
              the phone and dials.
```
Accepted. I won.
```
              Keller walks to the back hall turns into
              the doorway. It is an empty office. She
              turns around and strides back down the hall
              to find Harrington gone and his desk drawer
              open.
```

We walk down the hall to the Evidence Room. We walk in only to discover the Evidence Room is just an empty office. Our opinion might be, "Outraged, at being duped," by a childish trick. We walk back down the hall. Our new objective could be to "Give him hell." We could choose the transitive action verb, "Flatten Him." As in, flatten him with rage. We could want him to, "Beg forgiveness." We walk down the hall with a new objective.

```
                    HARRINGTON
              Just back there. End of
              the hall on the left.
              Tell Sergeant Powaschuck
              I sent you.
```
Relief. Maybe Harrington isn't so bad.
```
              He points down the back hall then picks up
              the phone and dials.
```
Accepted. I won.

Give him hell. *Beg forgiveness*
```
              Keller walks to the back hall turns into
              the doorway. It is an empty office. She
              turns around and strides back down the hall
              to find Harrington gone and his desk drawer
              open.
```
Flatten him. *Outraged, at being duped.*

Next is another action slug.

I sent you.
Relief. Maybe Harrington isn't so bad.
He points down the back hall then picks up
the phone and dials. *Accepted. I won.*

Give him Keller walks to the back hall turns into
hell, the doorway. It is an empty office. She *Flatten him.*
Beg turns around and strides back down the hall
forgiveness to find Harrington gone and his desk drawer
open. *Outraged, at being duped.*
The squad room door swings shut.

Off of Keller.

Harrington has taken off. The door is swinging shut, adding insult to injury. Our opinion could be "Livid," at being ditched. Livid is good because it is a quiet, cold rage- a good cap for the end of the scene. "Off of Keller" means that the writer is indicating that the scene should conclude with a shot of Keller's reaction. That being the case, it might spice things up for that reaction shot, if we added a new objective. "Revenge." We could add a transitive action verb like, "Ruin him." Maybe we want him to "Cry." This strong choice can really add a lot to the capper/reaction shot. It does not have to be our objective in the next scene, just in this moment. In a moment of rage, we mostly don't follow through with our initial decisions, thankfully.

I sent you.
Relief. Maybe Harrington isn't so bad.
He points down the back hall then picks up
the phone and dials. *Accepted. I won.*

Give him Keller walks to the back hall turns into
hell, the doorway. It is an empty office. She *Flatten him.*
Beg turns around and strides back down the hall
forgiveness to find Harrington gone and his desk drawer
open. *Outraged, at being duped.*
Revenge The squad room door swings shut. *Ruin him.*
Cry. Off of Keller. *Livid*

It's important to go over your script many times. Don't carve your first notes in stone. You may decide to refine opinions, objectives and tactics as you go. You might even change your mind entirely. On the day the director may change their mind so be open to change as always.

Now that we have completed this process, we should ask ourselves, what are the stakes in this scene? We know from the brief description of the character, that this is a big step in Keller's career. She is a detective promoted to Major Case Squad. It would probably take a great deal of ambition and hard work to get to Major Case Squad. She goes to great lengths to try and get along with her partner (Harrington), even putting up with his disrespect. Getting along with her fellow detectives would be very important for her to have an impact on the squad. I think we can assume her career is extremely important to her. Possibly the most important thing in her life. The stakes are professional but personally high.

Keller's ambition drives her actions throughout the script, this scene is from. She is trying to gain acceptance from Harrington but perhaps not for the best reasons. Keller is constantly wrestling with her ambition. She is tempted to do what is best for her career, even though it may not be the right thing to do. Keller's struggle with these competing desires is the inner tension of her character.

What kind of relationship do Keller and Harrington have? We could say, they are like competitive siblings.

You can see from one scene, there is enough information to understand the character we are playing:

- What she is trying to get

- Why she is trying to get it

- What are her obstacles

- How she is trying to get it

- Her opinion of her partner

- The relationship with her partner

- Plus, we have shed a little light on her inner tension. Not just in the scene but in the entire story.

Now that we have done the work of preparation, we are ready to perform. However, when we perform the scene, we must let go of all our preparation. I know letting it go sounds crazy, but we cannot hold onto the preparation and execute it like a set of instructions. If we do, our acting will seem contrived and completely unnatural. Let it go and trust your feelings. Just do the scene and try to get what you want. Trust yourself to get it right. Trusting yourself is the most important step in becoming consistently good as an actor. It is the hardest thing to do. It will take a while to get there, but you will make it. A good way to think of it is: Getting out of your brain's way. Because you prepped, your brain knows what to do. Trust it to do its job. Think of scene/script analysis as understanding the scene/script, rather than as a set of instructions. Once this understanding is accomplished. Commit and leap into the scene with gusto.

I know all this analysis seems complicated and not always obvious, but you will get better at this the more you do it. Something that always helps is to expand your vocabulary. The more words you know; the more tools you have to be specific with opinions, objectives and tactics. If you read a script and come across a word you do not know, look it up. The meaning of a word can change a scene. Also, don't be afraid to use a thesaurus to find more specific words.

Taking Direction

Often when filming a scene, you will receive direction that is vague or confusing. It is important to note that most directors are not actors and don't understand the jargon of acting. If a director tells you they want it bigger or more intense, you must translate what they are saying so you can deliver what they need. You could alter your performance to meet the director's needs, by changing the stakes of the scene, or a change in tactics, or changing your opinion. If in a scene, someone angers you and the director wants it bigger: Try changing your opinion of that character. Instead of being insulted, try degraded. This will raise the stakes and emotional intensity. Make your objective to hurt them. Change your tactics from humbling them to humiliating them. If the director wants it softer (or less big), maybe make your opinion about being hurt, change your objective to making them feel like you do, and your tactic to humbling them. You see how you can tweak the elements of your scene analysis by degrees and change the scene dramatically. Try practicing these techniques with actor friends or in a scene work class. Eventually you will be able to it without even thinking.

Directors and casting agents remember actors that can take direction well. Remember: Drama is a collaborative affair, and you must trust the director's vision, just like you trust another actor. Even if you disagree with the direction, just try it their way and if it does not work, usually they will see it. As actors it is our job to say yes to direction and make it work to the best of our abilities, however you should not be afraid to ask the director questions. Just do it respectfully and be open to trying it another way.

ADVANCED CONCEPTS IN ACTING

Layering Your Performance/Finding The Inner Tension

No character is just one thing. A thug is not just a thug. A professor is not just a professor. Your character must be a person, with all the complications of a person. We are a human first. Figure out who your character is as a human. Then ask yourself what they do for a living? What are their obsessions? What are their passions? What has happened in their life to get them to where they are? Figure out in what order these things are prioritized. Is their job more important than family? If so, why? Is it about ambition, or just the love of their job? You see how subtle you can get. These layers will be apparent in the text. It will usually be there in the objectives of the character. Understanding the layers of the character can create internal tension in the character.

A good example of this is Captain Picard on *Star Trek: The Next Generation*. Captain Picard is committed to being a Starfleet captain. However, there are several episodes where he considers having another kind of life. He explores romance and the possibilities of family. Even encountering aliens that trick him into believing he has lived a whole other life, with a wife and kids. He then must face his choices in life and wonder if he made the right ones. We call this internal conflict "inner tension" or "layers." This inner tension within the character makes for a much more interesting performance.

We love conflicted characters because we relate to them. We all have second thoughts about our lives, regrets about choices made or paths not taken. Sometimes we are simply confused about who we are. We may have moral dilemmas. We may want things that are not good for us. Or we may have to choose between two things that mean a great deal to us. A large part of life and drama is figuring out these questions.

In the classic film *Casablanca*, Humphrey Bogart and Ingrid Bergman must choose between love and duty. Bogart plays a cynical night club owner who does not seem to have a patriotic bone in his body. Bergman is an idealist who is married to an important resistance leader, fleeing the Nazis in World War II. Bogart and Bergman were lovers once and still have great passion for each other. She tries to convince Bogart to help them escape the Nazis. Bogart wants Bergman to stay with him. Bergman feels she must go with her husband but in the end succumbs to passion. Then something unexpected happens and Bogart's long buried idealism comes back to the surface. He decides he cannot be with her. Her husband's work is too important, and he needs Bergman more than Bogart does. This realization leads to a famous climactic ending where Bogart tells Bergman he must let her go. It is one of the best climactic scenes ever. The reason this movie is so popular is that the characters are so human. They are complex. They can be selfish and selfless too. It is a contradiction, but we humans are full of contradictions. If you find the contradiction, you find the inner tension, and it can make a performance great.

Sorry to use another *Star Trek* example but here goes: Captain Kirk is often stereotyped as a ladies' man. However, if you watch the whole series, you will see that he is a passionate character, that falls in love a little too easily. The captain in him must often reassert itself to keep his desires in check. It is clear he is attracted to Yeoman Janis Rand, but he can never express this attraction because he holds the responsibility of command. There must always be distance between him and everyone in his crew. This   distance creates an inner tension. He is human but also a captain.

Galadriel, in *Lord of The Rings* is a noble woman who leads her people against a power-hungry Dark Lord. In order to fight him, she must desire to be strong, to be powerful. When Frodo offers her the One Ring of Power, the most powerful weapon on earth, she is tempted; she could defeat the Dark Lord; she imagines all the good she might do with such power. She realizes though, that she would be corrupted and become evil herself. But she is tempted. This temptation creates an inner tension in her. If you can find the layers in the characters that are not explicitly expressed in the text, you can add a whole new dimension to the character and make the film or television show a lot more interesting.

Subtext

Subtext is all about what is really going on in a scene. You can get a scene where the two characters in it are being nice and polite to each other. A nice married couple talking about the weather; a perfectly pleasant conversation. But if we know that one of them found out the other was cheating on him or her, in the previous scene, this scene then takes on a whole new dimension.

The words in the scene do not match the characters opinions, objectives, and reactions. There could be real venom behind the words, or great hurt. Probably both. In a scene like this one you must figure out how that character feels, and try to cover it up, yet allow the audience to see it as well. Have the character's real reactions, but then try and hide them from the other character. The audience will sense the underlying tone and realize there is more going on beneath the surface.

Most well written scenes do have subtext. It is always the thing that is not being said and yet hangs in the air between the characters.

Emotional Preparation

Sometimes it may be necessary to prepare yourself for a particularly emotional scene. One technique I use is to put yourself through the scene in your head and allow yourself to feel everything the character feels. This technique will warm you up and allow you to get to the place you need to be at in the scene. The key to doing this technique, is doing your homework with the script. Find out what the character wants, what the stakes are, what their opinions are. Imagine yourself going through these things as the character and react naturally in your imagination. Then when you start the scene, let go of these feeling and do the scene as normal. Let go of your preparation and just get what the character wants.

You must be careful not to start the scene at the emotional climax, unless that is how the scene starts. We don't want the emotions to be at the top all the way through. We need arc in a scene. We need to start out one place and end up another. Remember to let go of preparation when you start.

Accents

Before we delve into accents: a warning. If you are going to do an accent for a role; do not focus only on the accent when you are acting. It will kill your performance. I was in a movie with a guy who had to do an accent. He was so focused on the accent, that he grooved his performance. He had rehearsed all his lines while mimicking the accent, then did all the other work of scene preparation. All that script analysis was a waste of time. His performance was locked in and devoid of any authenticity. It was all about faking his contrived accent. His character became his accent. Mimicry sounds like mimicry. It is not natural.

Before you even think about the accent, do your scene or script preparation. Figure out who your character is. Do your scene analysis. Do everything you would normally do. If the character comes from a different culture and mindset, then this mindset will be apparent in the text. Then learn the accent. Do not do an imitation.

I myself love to learn all about accents and different cultures. I go out of my way to know them. The important thing is to know the basics of the accent. Get them down so you can speak the accent in an easy manner. For instance, a British upper-class accent has some unique basics. The letter "A" is soft. It is said quickly and barely noticeable. The letter "R" before a consonant is again, almost silent. The consonant at the end of the word is short and sharp. My last name is Hart. An upper crust English person would pronounce it almost like the word, "Hot." Learn these characteristics of accents and then you will be able to say anything very naturally and authentically. It will become second nature if you do it enough. Practice talking like that in your everyday life. If that is too embarrassing, then read a random book aloud in the accent. If you can afford it, or get the production to pay for it, use a dialect/voice coach. There are also numerous YouTube videos about accents, which I have found helpful.

Don't tell your agent, a casting director or director, that you can do an accent. Not unless you are already familiar with the accent or are fully prepared to study the accent to the point that it is natural sounding.

COMEDY

The Basics of Comedy

Question: What are the differences between comedy and drama?

Answer: None. Comedy is drama, just with different stakes, different opinions, different objectives and different tactics.

When actors first try comedy, they almost always make the mistake of playing the comedy. They act wacky and over-act to try and make the scene ridiculous. It is vitally important in comedy to play a scene just like it is a drama. The only real difference is that you must raise the stakes and raise the level of commitment. Good comedy writers will make the scene funny for you. They will make it ridiculous. The hilarious part is not about you being wacky. The hilarious part comes in when your character is acting like the world is ending, if the dude they are crazy about rejects them, for example. In other words, their opinions, objectives, tactics and stakes are out of proportion with what is happening in the scene.

Comedy is deadly serious to the characters involved in the scene. In The Big Bang Theory, Sheldon is a character that is obsessed with having every little detail of his life in order. If one thing is out of place, he freaks out like it is the end of his world. For him chaos and uncertainty are a living hell and the solution to the problem of chaos, is order. Therefore, sitting in the same spot on the couch every time he is in the living room is not just about comfort, it is about preventing his world from flying apart. The stakes are out of proportion with what is happening. But that is what makes us all a little ridiculous. We often place undue importance on ordinary events.

Conversely, you could be playing a character that is doing something extraordinary but treating it in a completely casual way. In the Marvel Franchise, Tony Stark (Iron Man) has a casual and flippant way of understating enormous danger. He achieves this by having a casual tone or deflecting terror with a smart-alec joke. His opinion could be that he is terrified, but he covers it with a joke. The joke is the solution or tactic to solve the problem of being scared. His flippant sense of humor makes him charming while humanizing him.

Comic Timing

Timing is often said to be the most important thing in comedy. I have always found the phrase "comic timing," to be somewhat inadequate. It describes something we see from the outside rather than what is happening on the inside. It is like saying a car is fast without looking under the hood to find out why. Stakes, opinions, tactics, objectives are out of wack or elevated in comedy. So are our reactions. Allowing our reactions to set in, to be seen, becomes very important. Covering them does too. The audience must see these reactions. They must see the gears turning in the character's heads, as they find solutions to the ridiculous, yet high stakes situations they are in.

There is a great scene in the film *A Fish Called Wanda*, that exemplifies great comedic timing. Kevin Kline plays Otto, a cruel and arrogant hitman. Michael Palin plays Ken, a naive and sensitive guy, who loves animals. John Cleese plays Archie, a lawyer. All three of these characters have become embroiled in a jewel robbery and have all engaged in a complex double and triple cross. Each one wanting to get their hands on the jewels. The climax of the plot takes place at an airport; specifically, a runway under construction where there is wet cement everywhere. Otto has trapped Archie and is going to shoot him. Before Otto can shoot him though, Archie tells Otto to look behind him. Otto does so and does a double take when he sees Ken slowly coming toward him in a steamroller. Ken wants to kill Otto because Otto killed his beloved fish; named Wanda. He turns around to face the steam roller and starts laughing at Ken, making a joke about

Ken slowly trying to kill him. He is so confident he has time; Otto turns around to shoot Archie before he deals with Ken. It is then he realizes that when he laughed at Ken, he stepped off the plank he was standing on. Otto is now stuck in wet cement up to his ankles and cannot move. Realizing he is in trouble; he shoots at Ken. He misses and runs out of bullets. He looks at his gun, horrified at the ridiculous yet deadly predicament he is in. He tells Ken he was just kidding and offers him a deal to split the jewels. First offering him a fifty-fifty split. That doesn't work so he tries sixty-forty, then offers him the whole thing. Ken just keeps coming and Otto desperately tries to think of something else. He decides that Ken might be bluffing and arrogantly dares him to keep coming, declaring that Ken does not have the guts. Ken just shouts, "Revenge!" and keeps coming. Otto instantly realizes that his taunts are not working and admits, "OK, you've got the guts!" then desperately switches gears again and tries finally to apologize for killing Wanda but his arrogance and disdain for Ken is so intense his apology comes off very insincere and Ken just runs him over.

The comic timing is not about time. It is NOT about counting off a pre-set amount of seconds before reacting. It is about seeing Otto's thought process, reflected in his actions. When he does the double take, we see two different opinions. The first time he looks he sees a steamroller moving slowly towards him and thinks nothing of it. Otto turns his attention back to killing Archie. Then he realizes that Ken is driving the steamroller and looks back again utterly perplexed. This is what we mean by timing. It is not that Kevin Kline (Otto) took a certain amount of time, it is that he had clearly two different reactions and we saw the change as he looked back the second time. In every beat of the scene, we see Otto going through a thought process. He has opinions and then recognizes his obstacles and tries to find solutions to those obstacles. His objective is to stop Ken from killing him and he switches gears several times trying to accomplish his goals. He goes from an opinion of arrogant disdain to horror in the space of a few moments. We see all his opinions, stakes, obstacles, objectives, and tactics play out in his head. These thoughts playing out, is the comic timing. Kevin Kline takes the "time" to have the thoughts and opinions of the character. The situation is hilarious, as written by the writers, but Kline really sells it with a very truthful performance. He is not a brilliant comedic actor, he is a brilliant actor, using all the tools we have already discussed in this book to do the scene. Kline won an Academy Award for that role. I highly suggest you watch *A Fish Called Wanda*. All the actors in it are great and they put on a comedy masterclass.

Final Thoughts on Comedy

You could write a whole book on comedy. I have given you enough to get started, though. Just remember, comedy is largely about the absurdity of humans. We all have this absurdity in us to a certain extent. Again, comedy is drama, but with different stakes, different opinions, different objectives and different tactics. Adjust these scene elements and you will find the comedy. Also remember, commitment, stakes and impulses are even more important in comedy.

TECHNICAL ASPECTS OF FILM ACTING

Differences Between Film and Theatre

The main difference between film and theatre is distance of course. In theatre you are far away from the audience. In theatre you must do all your physical actions in a way that are clear to an audience member sitting at the back of the theatre. Your voice must carry to the back of the theatre. In theatre you are taught a number of skills, to allow you to project. These skills, while necessary in theatre, will not serve you well in film. They will make you look like a crazy person. You will be talking way too loudly, enunciating way too much and your physical actions will be way over the top. Not good, unless that is who your character is.

Working With The Camera

In film, the camera is right there, seeing every little detail of your performance. Just having a thought in your head can be read on your face, in your eyes and the subtle mannerisms of your body. Accordingly, your acting must be more natural, more subtle. More like real life.

There is a contradiction in film. Though your performance must be more natural, the process of making film is quite unnatural. We don't get multiple takes in theatre. Because of the way camera angles work, sometimes you can't even look at the actor that you are in the scene with. Sometimes even your body must be contorted unnaturally, in order to be in the right position for the camera. There have been times when I have been acting against a green screen, while looking at a ping pong ball on the end of a stick, that represents a CGI monster to be added in post by the effects crew. In film and television, the key is to make something look natural, even though it is being shot in the most unnatural way possible.

Most of the time you will be acting in a medium shot (waist up) or a close up. That means that as an actor, you cannot simply move around as you wish on the set. You will have a box of space which you can move around in. You will have to consult with the cameraman and ask them how freely you can move within that box. If you don't stay in that box, you will move out of shot. Or you might be in a position where you're blocking in the background, something that needs to be seen. Even while in that box, it's important to understand that you cannot make wild or overly theatrical movements. Again, the trick here is to act as naturally as possible, in a completely unnatural situation. You need to watch things, like shifting on your feet unconsciously. Shifting your feet may move your body in a distracting way that does not play well on camera.

When you rehearse a scene prior to shooting, marks will be put down where your character stands. Sometimes a character will have multiple marks, if there is a lot of movement in the scene. It is important to hit these marks, so that the camera can match your movements. Sometimes they have to change the focus of the camera as you are moving. You may be required you to match your timings with the cameraman's. This timing is vitally important because you can ruin a really good take, if your timings are off, or if you're missing your marks, or if you're moving outside of shot. In theatre you have weeks of rehearsals to work out all the blocking for your play. Blocking is simply where you will be in the scene and when. In film, you work out this blocking usually less than half an hour before you're going to shoot it. It's important to pick these things up fast and to be able to adapt if the blocking is being changed, while you are shooting it. Last minute changes are extremely common in film and television. Changes can and are often made, from take to take.

Also, it is a good thing to keep in mind, that in wider shots your movements must be able to read on camera. Subtle eye movements may not be noticed. So, if you are changing your eye line to look at something or someone else, you may have to move your head for instance, rather than just moving your eyes. I know all of this is a lot to take in, but film and television is all about the details. It's also about collaborating with the crew and your fellow cast mates.

Be aware of lighting. If you move out of the light, then your face might move into a shadow and ruin the effect that the cinematographer and director are going for. Or worse you may block another actor's light and cast a shadow on them. Some actors get really annoyed at their light being blocked. A couple of times when I was a younger actor, I annoyed some older actors by stepping into their light during a scene. If you want to avoid a testy rebuke from a surly old veteran actor, just make sure that you have good communication with the cameraman, cinematographer, and the director. Be aware of everything that is going on around you, especially during camera rehearsal. Don't be afraid to ask questions.

Working With Sound

Sound is extremely important in film and TV. We always assume that the visual is the most important part of film and TV, but if no one can hear what you are saying, it will not matter how good you look saying it.

Traditionally sound is recorded by boom mics. A microphone attached to a long pole. It is a directional mic pointing down at the actors from above their heads; held up by a person with strong arms (boom operators). As recording devices became smaller and more advanced, wireless body mics started to be used. Usually both boom and wireless mics are used today. When you arrive on set to shoot your scene, a sound person will rig you for sound. They will hide a wireless mic in your costume. It might be taped to you on the inside of your shirt. That is most common. It is a good idea to move your body around, after being mic'd just to test if your clothes are going to scrape up against the mic. Usually, the sound person will make sure your clothes are not scraping the mic but test it if they do not. It is your voice that will suffer if you don't test it.

Something you must learn is to keep your voice within a certain volume range. If you are too soft, your voice will not be heard. If you are too loud, your voice will "clip the audio." Clipping the audio is when your voice goes beyond the recordable range of the mic. Your voice will be distorted. It will sound just awful and cause the sound engineer to tear their hair out in postproduction, trying to fix it.

The sound is constantly monitored during the shoot by a sound mixer. They monitor the sound to catch clothing noises or clipping or lines that are delivered too low. This is not a perfect process and sound issues still make it to postproduction sometimes. Also, you don't want to be that person who screws up a perfect take because you were too loud or soft.

Also, it is important not to talk over the other actors lines unless you are directed to do so.

When the director says action, if you are the first actor with dialogue, then wait a couple of seconds before starting. It gives the editor some leeway in post.

Continuity

Continuity is very important. Continuity is just making sure everything matches and everything is consistent.

The most famous example of a continuity error is in the movie Pretty Woman. Julia Robert's and Richard Gere's characters are having a conversation over breakfast. In one shot Julia Roberts holds a croissant in her hand. It cuts to Richard Gere, and he says his line. It cuts back to Julia Roberts, and she is holding a pancake and not a croissant. These two shots of Julia Roberts were from different takes. At some point they had run out of croissants, or she just grabbed a pancake by mistake. Whatever the reason, there is a discontinuity between the two takes. This discontinuity can take the audience out of the story if it is too noticeable.

Continuity can also take the form of making sure your physical action is consistent. Editors will often cut from one angle to another. Each of these angles is shot separately, unless you are in a multiple camera shoot. Mostly it is one angle at a time in film. Your action must be consistent. If you miss your mark, you may appear to jump across the room when the editor cuts to another angle. Nothing will frustrate an editor more and potentially ruin a beautiful moment in the film.

It is also important to make your dialogue match as much as possible. If the editor cuts to you in mid-sentence and your words don't make any sense because you said different words, or said the words in the wrong order, it will again potentially ruin a good moment in the film.

Continuity does not mean that you should deliver the exact same performance over and over. Follow your instincts and impulses for each take. Directors often don't want a duplicate performance from take to take. It gives them options in the edit if you discover new things in the moment, in each take and shot. Different takes and shots just have to technically match.

My Most Challenging Technical Experience

To give you an idea of how technical and awkward film can be, I will tell you a story. On a series once, a western, I was required to ride a horse. The idea was that the two heroes in the series were chasing me down to find out what I knew about a murder. I of course lied when they asked me if I could ride a horse. I then went out and learned basic horse riding, at the cost of a few hundred dollars. I was really pumped to actually be in a western and gallop on a horse. When I arrived on set the director had decided he wanted to go another way. Instead, I had to run through a marsh with really rigid hip waders on, under my costume, with our heroes chasing me. The boots of the hip waders were always causing me to trip and fall. I had to work very hard to not trip but also to look like I was running for my life, with little regard for where my feet were falling. I could not look down because it would look strange. I had to also really shove the reeds out of the way, really dramatically, so it would look good on the camera that was shooting the wide shot- over the reeds. I had to do all this without looking like I was taking any care to really shove them out of the way, for the camera shooting tight on me. I then had to run out of the marsh up a steep embankment. At the top, another hero waited to apprehend me with a gun. When this hero stopped me, I had stop in these awkward, inflexible hip waders as if on a dime, on a greater that 60-degree incline. I had to hit the exact mark, every time, to be in the tight closeup and not shift on my feet in any way, or I would move out of shot. I had to do the whole thing in one go. They had three cameras so they could shoot it all in one. I did this take, after take, after take. Needless to say, I fell face down in the water a lot. I wish I had refused the safety conscious crew, who made me put the hip waders on, because they were seriously unsafe and painful. Somehow, I made all this work in at least one take out of the many we shot. The final product looked good and natural but was exhausting, miserable and wet to do. All this technical attention is the price of film acting. Now just imagine doing something like Matt Damon does: acting while fighting someone on the edge of a roof top. We often take for granted how difficult and complicated acting on camera can be, particularly when a great actor makes it look so easy.

Keeping Your Energy Levels Up

There is another hazard in film and television. Waiting on set for hours can drain the energy out of you. You can wind up waiting for hours before they shoot your scene. Often there are long waits between scenes. There are even long waits between shots as the crew resets all the lighting. When these pauses happen, find some way to keep your energy levels up.

Keeping your energy up is easier said than done. I was in a scene on a movie, shooting on the hottest day in 100 years. I had to wait 13 hours to shoot my scene and when they finally got to it, the first take was terrible. My words literally died in my throat. Keep your electrolytes up. Keep hydrated and don't take long naps. Before you go to set, listen to some energetic music and sing along with it. Talk to people. Do a little dance routine or exercise to get the juices flowing again. Just don't sweat in your costume too much.

Final Thoughts on The Technical Stuff and Film vs. Theatre

The bottom line is that theatre will always have a more organic feel to it. It will always be more enjoyable in the moment. With film you are often not able to enjoy it, until you see the final product. I strongly suggest you do both film and theatre. Film and TV gigs can be scarce. Theatre can fill in the gaps and it can help you reconnect with the sheer joy of acting. It will remind you why we go through all the hard work to become a good actor. In theatre you get weeks of rehearsal time to connect and bond with the other actors. You also get many performances. In film and TV, you will be playing small parts a lot. Usually, you show up, get into costume and make up and then sit for hours until they call you to set. The director says hi, you rehearse once or twice and then shoot it in a couple of takes and you are done. It can be very anti-climactic when you walk off a set at 4am, after waiting many hours to do your one line. Of course, the larger the role, the more satisfying it will be.

I am not telling you these stories to deter you. I tell them so you know what you are getting into and are prepared. Film, when it is done well can be an intimate and transforming experience. You can be a part of something wonderful that is preserved forever on film.

HOW A SCENE IS SHOT

Each film and TV show is different. How they are shot can vary depending on the style the Director and Director of Photography have agreed upon. Some shows have a traditional format for shooting.

- Traditionally film is shot on a single camera. Shooting one angle or shot at a time. A wide shot of the scene is shot, then coverage (or close ups) of each actor. Though sometimes, the coverage may be shot at multiple angles for each actor. If the production has multiple cameras, they might shoot multiple different angles at one time.

- Sitcoms are shot with a three-camera set up. They are filmed almost like a play, in front of a studio audience. One camera gets the wide shot of the whole scene. The other two get close ups or mid-shots of the actors. Although this may vary. The Office was shot in a one camera set up, like a feature film.

- Dramatic TV is mostly shot like a film. The closeups though are often shot tighter.

Below is how an actor might experience a day of shooting:

1. Arrive on location, on time. Timings are very important on a set as time is money. A big budget film could be burning thousands of dollars an hour.

2. Report to the circus. The circus is a staging area for the crew. You as an actor would report to the 2nd AD (Assistant Director) in the

main trailer, where their office is. They will direct you to your dressing room. Don't expect anything fancy.

3. A PA (Production Assistant) will come and get you when wardrobe is free to take care of you. You will go to their trailer, and they will outfit you. You may have already had a fitting for the costume on another day. Often the costume will just be delivered to your door if it requires no further adjustment.

4. Once you have changed, a PA will eventually knock on your door and take you to hair and make up. Once done there, you will go back to your dressing room.

5. Then wait. You may be stuck in your dressing room for an indeterminate time. Since you are being paid by the day, it makes sense to keep you hanging around. Also, they never really know just how long it will be until they get to your scene. If you need to stretch your legs, always let the PA know where you are going. They could summon you to set at a moment's notice. The longest I ever waited to be used was 21 hours. That is rare but it happens. It was a higher budget movie, and it was the last day of shooting. They were way behind schedule. So, bring a book, a computer, anything to amuse yourself. Music is good. It keeps the energy levels up. Run your lines and stay fresh.

6. You will be called to set eventually, and you will block and rehearse the scene. Rehearsal is usually done off to the side of the set, with the director and other actors, as the crew is setting up for the scene. Everything in film and TV is about efficiency.

7. The crew will eventually finish setting up and you will do a camera blocking and camera rehearsal. Camera rehearsal is the time to ask questions of the camera operator or the DOP, concerning things like what your box is. Be aware of lighting so you don't move out of the light or block anyone else's. They will put tape marks on the ground to tell you where to stand. You may have multiple in a scene, so make sure you pay attention when they explain them to you. A wireless mic may be put on you- hidden from view of course- usually under your shirt.

8. Eventually the 1st AD (Assistant Director) will call out, "Finals!" Make up, hair and wardrobe will finish giving you the once over and make final adjustments.

9. The 1st AD will shout out "Lock it up!" This means that all work on set should cease as they are ready to shoot. You should be on your first position or mark at this point.

10. The 1st AD will shout, "Quiet on the set!" Everyone will be absolutely quiet at this point.

11. The camera man will shout, "Speeding!" This means that the camera is recording.

12. The sound man will shout, "Sound speeding!" meaning the sound is recording.

13. The 1st AD will shout, "Rolling!" Others in the crew will repeat "rolling" to make sure everyone hears it.

14. The director will then say "Action."

15. The 1st AD may also shout "Action!"

16. Then you start acting.

17. They will shoot a wide shot usually at first. Usually, they will only do one or two takes of a wide shot.

18. When you are done someone will shout, "Moving in!" or something like that, to let everyone know they are resetting the cameras, lights and set for close ups.

19. How many takes they do of any one coverage depends on how much budget they have and how satisfied the director is. The shots may vary: Sometimes they will do a two shot of the actors; Sometimes they may simply shoot the scene wide. There are always exceptions.

20. Once the first close up is done, someone will shout, "Turning around!" This means they are turning the cameras and lights around to shoot the coverage on one of the other actors.

21. Once the crew is done turning around, there will be a camera rehearsal, maybe some blocking or adjustments to blocking.

22. Then rinse and repeat. They will shoot the coverage of the other actor or actors. They may adjust angles or do different kinds of coverage, it just depends.

23. Eventually the scene will be finished when the director is satisfied and the 1st AD will shout, "Checking the gate," meaning they are just making sure they have everything they need. In the old days they used to check the gate on the camera frame, to make sure there was no hair or dust in it.

24. Shortly after checking the gate, the 1st AD will shout, "Moving on!" This means they will tear down and set up for the next scene. Or they will wrap for the day, depending on time.

If you have more scenes or more days on set, it will go just like what I have described above. Ideally, a film crew is a well-oiled machine. However, stuff often gets delayed, or things go wrong. In those circumstances, just be patient. If people are stressed and tempers are running high, just be quiet and concern yourself with yourself. Stay in the moment, stay in the scene. It is always good to be quiet on set. The director and all the ADs have a million things going through their heads. They need to focus. Film is a details business.

Be nice and respectful to the crew. From the director on down to production assistants. Crew make you look good, sound good and keep you fed. They bust their asses for 10 to 14 hours and come back for more the next day. Film and TV could not happen without them. Always remember that.

AUDITIONS

The Basics

Many people (usually those trying to sell you a spot in their audition workshop) will tell you that auditioning and performing are radically different. They are not. You do the same prep that you do for any scene or script. The differences are in the physical execution. You will be in a small plain room, standing on a single mark. There will be a camera guy and a casting director. Sometimes the director will be present, depending on the size of the role. Say hi, ask questions if you have any but try and get down to business. Try to stay in character as you go in and during the whole audition and as you leave as well. I find staying in character helps keep you in the moment and helps convince a director. Some directors don't trust acting. They like to believe you are that character.

Mostly you will be unable to do much in the way of physical action. In an audition you are reading to a reader, who most of the time will not be an actor. They may or may not give you any good reactions or opinions to work with. Imagination is key in an audition. Do your moment before and start the scene as normal. If you are speaking to multiple characters, address your dialogue to the single reader. Sometimes they may have a second reader but not usually. Usually there is a chair if your character is sitting in the scene. It is usually OK to stand or sit down during the audition but ask first if that is OK. The camera man will need to know. If you have physical action, then bring it down so that you don't step out of the shot. You will have to adapt. However, there is the odd audition where it is all or mostly physical action. In that case, ask the casting director if they want to see it in the audition. They usually explain in the casting notice, if they want specific physical action. Prepare to do it either way, they may change their mind in the audition. Ask questions if there is confusion. Or ask your agent to ask them before the audition.

If the script requires that the performance have props, then you will have to use your judgment. I brought a cigar to an audition as the character was smoking one in the scene. I felt it was necessary to the scene, just don't light a cigar or cigarette or anything with a flame. The script required a gun as well. Don't bring a prop or toy gun to an audition. A gun may cause problems especially if they are not ready for it. I would put that on the "never-do" list. Just use your finger or mime it.

Costumes should not be elaborate. Just dress in something that looks vaguely like the one you might wear in the scene. Businessperson or lawyer, a suit. For a uniformed cop role, black trousers and a blue shirt. For a pirate, a puffy dress shirt. You get the idea.

Do your scene as prepared but be adaptable. You may walk into a less-than ideal audition situation. I had a reader once blast through the dialogue so fast, I could not even react to it. If that happens to you, politely ask to do it again slower. The reader may be bad so you may have to imagine the reactions and energy they are giving you. Don't do that on set if you get the part. React to the actor you will be working with.

You are going to be in a room full of people who have been watching the same auditions all day long. After a while they are going to just want to get through it. You must come pumped full of energy and be in the moment to grab their attention. Don't let their lack of energy and the stuffiness of the room rub off on you. As actors we often mirror the energy and mood of the environment we are in, so be aware that you must resist that urge in an audition.

Always come with a paper copy of the script in your back pocket in case you have to refer to it. Don't read from it unless it is absolutely necessary. Know your lines as well as you can. Not knowing your lines is a major turn off in an audition. It can be a challenge sometimes though. I once had four hours notice for an audition and had to memorize fourteen pages of dialogue for three different characters. I was still madly cramming the lines in my brain on the subway ride to the audition space. It was not a great audition, but I got through it. If you forget a line, try to say something close to it. If you prepare well, you will know the thoughts behind the words and be able to improvise something. Only refer to your script if you absolutely have to.

Always have a hard copy of your resume and head shot with you. A lot of casting directors use digital ones now, but it does not hurt to be prepared.

Call Backs

You may have heard actors refer to "call backs." The call back audition is usually a second or third audition. They usually happen when directors and producers are having trouble deciding between two actors. They want you to audition again to try and break the tie. Sometimes there will be notes from them but sometimes not. How to approach them is tricky. You can add to your performance but that runs the risk of changing what they liked about the first audition. But not adding may be a risk too. Sometimes your performance may be just right and there is simply nothing to add. You may wreck your performance by trying too hard. My general advice is do what you did in the first audition, unless you find a subtle layer too add in that does not alter the performance much. Often the director and/or the producers are just having a hard time choosing. Stick with what worked the first time unless they give you notes. Don't be afraid to ask in the audition if they are looking for something more. You can also ask your agent to inquire. That would probably be the best route

Self-Taped Video Auditions

Self-taped video auditions are a big thing now. When they first started, we were told that they would allow us to audition for stuff all over the world, through the magic of the internet. Most actors are auditioning for smaller parts that are tied to a local tax credit. If a production hires a local actor, then they get a tax break from the government. What video auditions are really about is saving the cost of having a casting director, renting a space and hiring a camera operator and a reader. It is much easier and cheaper to have the actors absorb the cost. For some a self-taped audition might be better, as you have the option to send your best take. It can be convenient as they can be filmed on a smart phone, most being more than good enough for the task nowadays. However, if you are auditioning a lot, it may be tricky to find a friend to help you as you still need a reader. I have had years where I had almost a hundred auditions. I spent a couple of thousand dollars on video auditions in those years. If you have to pay a professional to help you do it, the costs can add up. Be prepared for this expense. Or make sure you have lots of friends who can help you.

Audition Waiting Rooms

A tip for going to auditions: When you are in the waiting room before you audition, try to stay focused. Don't engage in too much conversation with the other actors there. There is an etiquette to audition waiting rooms. If some other actor is talking your ear off, then don't be afraid to ask them to stop. Just politely say you are trying to focus on your audition. Some actors are just chatty, others are trying to throw off their competition.

Final Thoughts On Auditions

It is important not to get psyched out by the pressure of auditioning. Embrace the pressure and use it as rocket fuel. Also, remember that everyone in that audition room wants you to succeed. No one goes to the trouble of auditioning you just to watch you fail.

Lastly, I would like to say, have fun at your auditions. Enjoy the performance, because if you do not, odds are those watching it won't enjoy it either. You will be acting, even if it is just an audition, and that is always a positive. As soon as your audition is over, go do something else. Do not obsess over how well you did. If you feel you made a real mistake in the audition, acknowledge it and move on. You will audition a lot and getting your hopes up too much will make you bitterly disappointed. Just try and do your best each time and then move onto the next thing. Mostly you will never be informed that you did not get the role. Do not wait by the phone. Find something positive you did in the audition and focus on that.

THE BUSINESS CALLED SHOW

Casting

Something you need to take to heart about this business, is that you will be typecast. Typecasting will be based on your physical look, your personal energy and charisma. We all like to think of Hollywood as the place where dreams are made. It is also a business. Most movies and television series are being made to appeal to the widest possible audience, because film and TV making is a very risky business. It is very expensive, and investors want to see a return on their investment. Often that means the safest choice is the choice that is made by directors, writers and producers.

The "safest choice" is also true for casting. The effect of the "safest choice" means that they are not going to cast people that go against type. In other words, they are going to be casting a guy who looks like a cop, to play a cop. Typecasting even happens at the top of the business. Clint Eastwood plays the anti-heroes because he's kind of got a rough, desperate look to him. Tom Cruise gets cast as the smart-alec hotshot, because he looks like a smart-alec hotshot. Usually, these actors also naturally exude the energy of that type of character. There are occasions where some actors are cast in order to transform into the character. These occasions are rare and usually only happen to people at the very top of the business. This is a tough pill to swallow for a lot of actors, but it's just how the business works. Opportunities to play different roles will eventually come along. But when you are starting out don't worry about being typecast, it happens to all of us.

Career Advice

I don't like to tell people what to do. Every time in my life that I have taken someone else's advice to heart, it has not worked out well for me. The only advice I have to offer, is the advice I started with at the beginning of this book. Find out what you want, then figure out how to get it. The truth is that the life of most actors is hard. You will be poor, mostly rejected, and if not careful, you might be exploited. That does not mean you can't have a deeply satisfying career. The point of acting is to create amazing moments on camera or stage.

Your career will have ups and downs. Even big stars often wait long periods of time, before doing any work that they find gratifying. But when you do find that gem of a project that you are lucky enough to be cast in, you will feel like you have wings... At least until you are out of work again.

Acting is not just a career; it is a lifestyle. It demands that you be available all the time to do auditions and prepare for them. You must find some way to make this crazy schedule work economically. You must find a regular job that will both support you and give you time to audition and hopefully act. You must also combat the rejection and hopelessness that can come with it. You must decide what you want. Ask yourself some questions, and be honest with yourself:

- Can I live a life of poverty as long as I am able to act?

- How much rejection can I take?

- Will I be happy living this life in the long run?

- Can I go sometimes a year or more, without being cast in something?

It is important to ask these questions. Then you can make a plan. I know some actors who do theatre and are character actors in film. They are not wealthy and live paycheck to paycheck, but they are doing what they love. For others, that paycheck to paycheck lifestyle is not for them. They give themselves a time limit to start booking work regularly and quit if they do not hit their timeline. I know others who hold down full-time jobs and act in Indie films on the side. I know people who act in smaller markets, hold down full-time jobs and audition for large feature films when they come to town. They can audition while working full-time because auditions in these small markets are rarer, and they don't need to be as available.

Ideally you want to be able to book enough acting work that you can support yourself. Unfortunately acting does not always pay the bills, or it might happen only for short stretches of time. Decide what you can tolerate and what you can't. It is a personal choice. You must decide how you want to live your life.

If you decide you want to commit to film as a career and you want to go for larger roles, then the logical next step is to go to a larger market. It is very difficult to make a living off of acting in smaller markets like say Toronto. Most of the larger roles in North America are cast out of either Los Angeles or New York. In the UK it would be London. Larger markets are of course riskier than smaller markets, so be prepared to endure more rejection and more financial strain before success comes. It may profit you to build a bit of a resume in a smaller market while you are learning to act. Then make the jump to Hollywood. It may give you an edge. If acting at the top of the business is your dream, fully commit to your career and commit to being the best actor you can be. Remember, there is no try. Do or do not.

Even being a great success in this industry can be fraught with pitfalls. Big name A-listers often are so busy they never see their family and friends. Working back-to-back movies, 12-14 hours a day, all over the world is enough to put strain on the strongest of relationships. Be sure that is the life you want.

As you age, the type of roles you will get will change. You will get smaller roles, more character-type roles, that pay less. It can also happen that your look or character type just falls out of fashion and show business is just done with you. It can be a cruel business and you must try to find an equilibrium that you can live with.

I am not trying to scare you off with my dire warnings. I just want to be honest to those of you just starting out, so you know what you are in for. Ultimately, only you can know what you want. Only experience in the business can really inform your decisions.

The Brad Pittiest

For every Brad Pitt there are thousands of Brad Pitt types that don't make it that big. Brad Pitt sat at the top of his category of actor in Hollywood because he was the Brad Pittiest of all Brad Pitts. What I mean by that is, he looked the most like the handsome cool guy character he often plays. He naturally exudes that energy. Sometimes you can be good but get stuck behind another actor whom they just like more. For years there was one actor whom I was always in competition with. I came in second to him for years, every time I auditioned. It was terrible. But that is the way Film and TV works. There are so many people chasing the same role that they can find just the right kind of actor they are looking for. You may audition and do great; but then another actor walks in after you and is just as good as you but has blue eyes. The director could have imagined the character having blue eyes, and that tips it over the top. You are not really competing against other actors. You are competing against the image of the character the director and producers have in their minds.

I once auditioned for a small part as a moonshiner in a western series. It was such a well written part, with great dialogue. It was only one scene, but a great one. I prepared the crap out of that scene. I did so well in the audition, that I was brought back for a call back audition in front of the director, the producers and a whole slew of other people. There were like ten people in the room. They did something that they almost never do in an audition. They told me what they were looking for. They wanted a shorter, hairier, pot-bellied guy who looked more like the character. I was none of these things. However, they were impressed with my performance, so they gave me another chance. They told me I would really have to act the crap out of it. I did the audition and thought I did well but could see from the look in their eyes that it was not to be. The guy they cast was just the look I described. The story did have a happy ending for me. I was cast in a much larger part in the next episode of the series. One I was probably more suited for. Yet, that small part is the one that got away. One of my best auditions ever and yet I did not get it.

Agents

Getting an agent takes time. Build up your resume, go to acting classes and hone your craft. Along the way, keep submitting to agents. Act in anything you can get. Do lots of independent film. Just keep building that resume and submitting to agents. It is about putting in the time. It's about firing enough buckshot into the air. Eventually you will get one. Go to the local actor's union website and there is usually a list of credible agents. Just go down the list and don't be afraid to resubmit to an agent a second or third time. Show business is about persistence. Most agents have a website. They usually have specific submission guidelines. Follow these guidelines. Due to the volume of submissions they get, they will find any reason to reject a submission.

Headshots, Resumes and Demo Reels

If you want an agent to see what you can do, put together a demo reel. Choose 1-3 three different short scenes you have been in. Ones that really show your acting skills. You might have to ask the film makers for video or do a screen recording on your computer to get them. Below is a link to my demo reel to give you a sense of what they want.

https://vimeo.com/98222248

Make sure you have an up-to-date resume that is one page. See the back of the book for an example, an old resume of mine.

Have an up-to-date headshot. Do not go overboard with headshots. Sometimes when you are not booking work, you can drive yourself crazy obsessing about things like headshots. You can waste a lot of money reshooting them, in a desperate attempt to change your situation. They just have to look professional and look like you. There are lots of photographers who do them. Just use google to find one in your area or ask another actor who they used. Get new headshots every few years so they are current.

Final Thoughts on Career

Just act. Take whatever work you can get (short of something ex-
ploitive). Do lots of independent film. If you are not in an actor's union, then do lots of non-union stuff as well. Make friends in the industry. If you can't get cast in the film, then volunteer to help make the
film. It will give you industry experience and you can make connec-
tions. Your name will be in the film makers mind, and they may cast
you in something else down the line. Just try and always be involved
in doing stuff. Make projects with your fellow actors, even if they are
just short films. It will give you experience, and it is just fun to do. Of
course, I would suggest doing theatre. It is very satisfying and looks
good on your resume. Also casting people and directors go to see
plays. You can also build a reputation as a theatre actor that can help
you get film and television work. In short, just act whenever possible.

FINAL THOUGHTS

It is important as an actor to become a student of human nature. Art is about understanding ourselves, and the world around us. Endeavour to discover how human beings work. Try and discover what makes us all the same and what makes us all different. Get good at seeing the world from someone else's point of view. People sometimes have different opinions, feelings or beliefs than you do. Usually, they have reasons for these different outlooks on life. Find out what experiences in their life may have caused these different outlooks. Try not to be judgmental. When you get good at it, acting will not be a big mystery but a wonderful tool for understanding your fellow humans.

ACTOR CHEAT SHEETS
Scene/Script Analyses:

Find out what your character wants (objectives)

Assess your character's obstacles

Find out what your character's tactics are (solutions)

Imagine how you want the other characters to react to your tactics

Discover your character's opinions

Find the beat changes

Ask what the stakes are (what happens if they do not achieve their objectives)

Find out what their relationship is to the other characters

Find the inner tension in your character (layers)

Look for subtext

Make a backstory

Make a moment before

Know the thoughts behind the words

Then memorize

Performing:

Breathe and relax (be the calm before the storm)

Let go of your preparation

Connect with the other actors

Focus

Slip into your moment before

Act on impulse

Be in the moment

Focus on task

Then act

TRANSITIVE ACTION VERBS

accept	acknowledge	admit
aggravate	answer	ask
avoid	beat	bend
bless	bother	break
build	cancel	capture
carry	catch	change
chase	chastise	clean
collect	confess	comfort
contradict	convert	crack
dazzle	deceive	define
describe	destroy	discover
distinguish	drag	dress
dunk	edify	embarrass
embrace	enable	encourage
entertain	execute	enlist
fascinate	finish	follow
flick	forget	freeze
frighten	forgive	furnish
gather	grab	gras
grip	grease	handle
hang	head	highlight
honor	hurry	hurt
help	imitate	impress
indulge	insert	interest
inspect	interrupt	intimidate
involve	irritate	join
judge	keep	kill
kiss	knock	lead
leave	lighten	limit
link	load	love

lower	maintain	marry
massage	melt	mock
murder	notice	number
offend	order	paralyze
persuade	petrify	pierce
place	please	poison
possess	prepare	promise
protect	purchase	punch
puzzle	question	raise
reassure	recognize	refill
remind	remove	repel
ring	run	satisfy
scold	select	slap
soften	specify	spell
strike	surprise	switch
teach	taste	tickle
tighten	toast	transform
tweak	twist	turn
toss	try	underestimate
understand	unlock	unload
use	untie	upgrade
vilify	wake	want
warm	wash	warn
watch	wipe	wrack
wrap	wreck	

GLOSSARY OF FILM TERMS

Action- Start the scene.

Blocking- How the actors will move or where they physically will be on the set during the scene. Usually figured out in a rehearsal prior to shooting the scene.

Camera Speeding- Camera is rolling and recording. In the film days it meant the film reels were spinning.

Checking The Gate- The 1st AD shouts this when the director has determined they have finished shooting the scene. They are checking to see if the footage is good. In the days of film, they would literally check the gate of the camera to make sure there had not been dirt or hair in it.

Circus- The circus is the area where the production's trucks are all parked. All the departments have a truck, from electrical to camera to hair and makeup. Usually the circus is where your dressing room is, in a trailer. It is like the production Head Quarters.

Lock It Up- All work on set must cease, as we are about to shoot.

Marks- Marks are put on the ground to indicate where an actor stands or where you they will move to. Usually colored tape in a "T" shape.

Moving In- literally means they are moving the camera closer to the actor. Usually for a closeup.

Moving On- If the director is satisfied after checking the gate, then the 1st AD shouts "moving on." It means they are moving on to the next scene.

On The Day- Not a particular date or time, simply refers to "when we shoot the scene."

Picture Wrap- The production is wrapped. They have finished all shooting for the project.

Picture Wrap For (insert actors name here)- If an actor is wrapped or done all their scenes on the film, then this is shouted out by an AD, "That's a picture wrap on Tony Hart!" The crew usually claps.

Quiet On Set- Everybody, absolutely quiet.

Rolling- Means everything is speeding and we are ready to shoot.

Sound Speeding- sound is on and recording. In the old days of reel to reel recording it meant the reels were spinning.

Turning Around- Shouted to tell the crew that they are switching to another actor's coverage. Literally turning the lights and cameras around. Window Shot- Last shot of the day.

Wrap- Means the production is wrapped for the day.

WHO IS WHO ON A SET

Director- In charge of the films vision. Overall, a director is in charge of the shooting aspect of the production.

1st Assistant Director (1st AD)- They are the 2nd in command for the production. Makes everything happen that the director needs to happen. Directs extras.

2nd Assistant Director (2nd AD)- They handle the administrative aspects of a production. Usually have an office in a trailer at the circus.

3rd Assistant Director (3rd AD)- Is usually on set assisting 1st AD. Usually directs background extras.

DOP (Director of Photography)- Also referred to as the Cinematographer. They oversee the camera and lighting department on a shoot. They help the director bring their vision of how the film or tv show is shot, to fruition. In short, they will make you look good on film.

Camera Operator- The camera person. It is important to have good communication with them. They can tell you your box (how much room you have) and tell you how you can move around in the shot. Establish good communication with them.

Boom Operator- Boom Operators are part of the sound department and are called so as they hold a long boom. At the end of this boom is a mic. This is called the boom mic and is held just above the frame of the shot, above the actors' heads to pick up dialogue. They have strong arms.

PA (Production Assistant)- Often the person that escorts you around the circus and set. They make sure you are where you need to be when you need to be there. They also do a number of other jobs on set, everything from admin to traffic control.

Craft Services- Craft services or Crafty, provide food and refreshment on set. Bless them.

Hair and Make Up- They make you look good.

Wardrobe- They provide you with your costume.

Stand In- A stand in is someone employed by the film because they match an actor's general physical type. They are used for camera rehearsals mostly and work with the DOP and camera operators.

Extras (Background Performers)- Sometimes referred to as BG. They are non-speaking performers. They play the role of random people in the background. As an actor you will be interacting with a lot of them. They are crucial to building the world of the film.

There are many more crew people, too numerous to mention them all. Be nice to them all and remember they are part of a massive collaboration of creatives. They are every bit as crucial to a production as you are.

RESUME

TONY HART

555.555.5555
actor@beemail.com
23-64 Some St.
Town · Country
Postal Number

Union #: 05-555555 · Height: 6'1 · Weight: 185 lb · Hair: Copper/ Brown · Eyes: Blue

FILM/TELEVISION

Tales From The Loop	Actor	Amazon Studios
First Light	Actor	FL Film Productions
Killjoys	Actor	Killjoys II Productions
The Pinkertons	Large Principle	Buffalo Gals, Rosetta Media
Silent Night	Actor	Genre Co.
The Don Cherry Story	Actor	Blue Coach MB Prod.
Breakfast Television	Actor	Cititv
UFO Abductions: The Taking of Marty	Lead	Tony Hart
Cowboy Dreams	Principal	Two Lagoons Prod.
Mnemonic	Lead	Yerstory Prod.
Nobody	Principal	Nobody Productions
Bronzville	Principal	Caitlin Brown/ Independent
The River Knows	Lead	Yerstory Prod.
Innate	Principle	Bunky Blum Productions
A Fable About Beauty	Principal	Far Point Films
Watchmen Reward	Lead	Watchmen Productions
Any Winnipeg Street	Lead	Doug Livingston/Independent
ZBC Undeadline	Lead	Neural Networks Productions
Workaholic	Principle	Independent
Cry of The Sasquatch	Lead	Yerstory Prod.
His Father's Son	Lead	Neural Networks Productions
Reflections	Lead	Neural Networks Productions
Last Call	Principal	Emily Silver Prod.
Christmas Spirit	Lead	Tony Hart/ Independent
Diary of a Zombie	Lead	Tony Hart/ Independent
Last Chance	Actor	David Joseph/ Independent

COMMERCIALS

Travel Manitoba/ UN Fresh Water	Actor	Centric

THEATRE

Some Light Underground	Raphael	Theatre Incarnate/ Carol Shields Festival
The Hairy Ape	Long	Theatre Incarnate/ MTC O'neillFest

WEB SHOWS

Roomies	Principal	Yerstory Prod.
Radio Free Krakow	Principal	Rogue Nation

TRAINING

On Camera Acting	Pro Actors Lab - Marvin Hinz-Toronto
BA Theatre	University of Winnipeg with Per Brask, Doug Arrell, Blake Taylor
Film Acting	Jeff Skinner – Actors Training Center
Film Acting	Darcy Fehr – The Acting Studio Winnipeg
Voice Over Training	Jeff Skinner - Actors Training Centre

SPECIAL SKILLS

Canadian Armed Forces Infantry, Fire Arms Safety, Computers, Sailing, Canoeing, Astronomy, English Lit. BA, Journalism, Poker, Experience in Politics, Cross Country Skiing

ABOUT THE AUTHOR
Tony Hart

Tony Hart has acted across North America in film television and theatre.

This photo is Tony Hart in his dressing room, on the series The Pinkertons.

His IMDB page:

Tony Hart III

https://www.imdb.com/name/nm2714869/?ref_=fn_al_nm_4

His Demo Reel

https://vimeo.com/98222248

Manufactured by Amazon.ca
Bolton, ON

27982103R00050